CHRISTIAN WIVES

CHRISTIAN WIVES

*Women Behind the Evangelists
Reveal Their Faith in Modern Marriage*

James Schaffer

and

Colleen Todd

A DOLPHIN BOOK
Doubleday & Company, Inc.
Garden City, New York
1987

Library of Congress Cataloging-in-Publication Data

Schaffer, James.
Christian wives.

"A Dolphin book."
1. Evangelists' wives—United States—Biography.
2. Evangelists—United States.   I. Todd, Colleen.
II. Title.
BV3780.S33   1987   269′.2′0922 [B]   87–5291
ISBN 0-385-23581-X

Photographs in *Christian Wives* are compliments
of the respective ministries.

To my mother and father for teaching me
all that is good and true and lasting—and
for giving me a faith to live by.

JAMES SCHAFFER

For my mother, Claire Patnode, for her
patience and belief in me.

COLLEEN TODD

ACKNOWLEDGMENTS

Special thanks to Mr. Phil Cooke, who brought this writing team together and opened many doors for our interviews. Without him this book would not have been possible. Phil is the ever creative Director of Television for the Oral Roberts Ministries in Tulsa, Oklahoma.

James Schaffer offers a very special thank-you to his good friend Cheryl Clevenger, who provided encouragement and listened long-distance to his frustrations and triumphs as he traveled more than twenty thousand miles, coast to coast, conducting interviews. Deep appreciation is also due to Mr. Paul O. Sauerteig, his attorney and close friend, and to Mr. Sauerteig's secretary, Mari Bojrab, for her help with typing. Also, thanks to Paul Deane and the Reader's Services staff at the Allen County Public Library in Fort Wayne, Indiana, for their comprehensive research assistance.

Colleen Todd wishes to thank her coauthor, James Schaffer, for his unflagging labor and support over two years of research; Marla Cassi, her patient typist, for service above and beyond the call of duty; Tim Patnode, Ms. Todd's brother, for his encouragement; our editor at Dolphin/Doubleday, Jim Fitzgerald, for his undying patience; and Jane Brummitt, Antonia Boyle, Dawn Caden, Trena Clem, Tara Hansen, Sara Potter, Paulette Steves, and Marilyn Stapleton for their interest and support throughout this project.

Most of all we wish to thank the personal assistants and

executives of the seven ministries with whom we worked on a weekly basis for over a year. They willingly answered question after question and verified endless facts and quotes. Our thanks to our good friends at:

Heritage U.S.A. and the PTL Television Network
> Neil Eskelin, Executive Vice-President for Public Relations
> Bobbie Garn, Director of Tammy Bakker's television program, "Tammy's House Party"
> Carolyn Williams, Secretary to Tammy Bakker

The Jerry Falwell Ministries and "The Old Time Gospel Hour"
> Diane Whitehurst, Secretary to Jerry and Macel Falwell

The Billy Graham Evangelistic Association
> Evelyn Freeland, Secretary to Ruth Graham

The Rex Humbard Ministries
> Elizabeth Humbard Darling, Rex Humbard's daughter and Communications Executive for the Rex Humbard Ministries
> Jeannie Morris, Secretary to Maude Aimee and Rex Humbard

The Oral Roberts Evangelistic Association
> Dr. Jan Dargatz, Executive Vice-President for Creative Development
> Gwen Culver, Secretary to Evelyn and Oral Roberts

The Robert Schuller Ministries and "The Hour of Power"
> Pat Scannell, Secretary to Arvella Schuller
> Fred Southard, Executive Vice-President for "The Hour of Power"
> Marge Kelley, Secretary to Robert Schuller
> Colleen Johnson, Television Associate for Arvella Schuller

The Jimmy Swaggart Ministries
> Donnie Swaggart, son of the Reverend and Mrs. Swag-

gart, and Chief of Staff of the Jimmy Swaggart Ministries

Barbara Cline, Administrative Assistant for Frances Swaggart

CONTENTS

PREFACE

Love is the world's most powerful force. The second is commitment. When these two heartfelt forces meet, the union generated frequently brings about marriage.

The building of seven marriages, day after day and year after year, provides the stories of *Christian Wives*. They are stories rich in both love and commitment and in great faith —three powerful forces that intertwine in the lives of seven remarkable women.

The joy in these marriages is best represented, perhaps, in the lives of Dr. Billy Graham and his wife, Ruth Bell Graham. A New York *Times* columnist once referred to Dr. Graham and his wife as a "dazzling advertisement for the state of matrimony."

Or it may be found in the marriage of Oral and Evelyn Roberts, as Mrs. Roberts replies: "The Lord gave Oral the talent to do two things: the talent to preach and to love me." There is Arvella Schuller, who says she and her husband, Dr. Robert Schuller, are to this day "crazy in love," and the Falwells, who are totally committed to their children and to each other.

Today marriage is as popular as ever. Unfortunately, so is divorce. Far too frequently, when love grows dim, the result is divorce, which makes the marriages of these women—all of them mothers—cause for celebration.

Not that there isn't pain in their lives. There have been great loss and sadness: a son dead to apparent suicide; a daughter with an amputated leg . . . a grandchild with less than two days of life . . . another daughter and her husband tragically killed in a small-plane crash.

Far too often these women experienced deep mood swings brought about by loneliness and the repeated question of "Why?" when tragedy struck.

Yet if there was a time when commitment and love waned, there was always faith. It was that faith, a deep belief in a purpose bigger and more permanent than both of them, that keep these wives and husbands together.

As Maude Aimee Humbard said, "I never gave up because Rex has a destiny. From the time of Rex's birth, God planned a special place for him in the Kingdom." And Frances Swaggart commented, "The Lord said to me, '[Your husband] will not be just a pastor, he will not be just a preacher, he will not be just an evangelist. He has a special call.'"

Each of these marriages is based on that call and that commitment to faith. Certainly each woman would echo Ruth Graham's statement when she told us: "The heart of our marriage has been our mutual love for and commitment to Christ." Above all, that is the story of *Christian Wives* and the message these women want to share with you.

Almost every day, Tammy Bakker tells the twenty million viewers of the PTL Television Network: "You can make it. Yes you can. Don't you ever give up." If you, a friend, or a relative need to know that "you can make it"—if you need that encouragement—we hope you find it in the pages of *Christian Wives*. It is there to be found.

TAMMY FAYE BAKKER

I want to be remembered as someone who really cared. I'm just who I am. With me, what you see is what you get.

TAMMY BAKKER

It is nine o'clock on a Tuesday morning and people are already lining up for audience seats for the "Jim and Tammy Program," on the PTL network. There's a family from Little Rock, Arkansas, who has spent every vacation for the last four years right here at the third largest tourist attraction in the United States, Heritage USA. Standing in line behind them is a couple from Great Neck, New York. "It's so pretty down here," says the wife, referring to the Charlotte, North Carolina, area, "that I wouldn't mind retiring here in a few years."

Ask the couple from New York or the family from Arkansas what the attraction is and you may get different answers. But ask them who they hope to see during today's PTL taping and you'll get the same response: Tammy.

Tammy is Tammy Faye Bakker, also known as Mrs. Jim Bakker, the popular hostess of PTL and co-partner with her husband Jim of the successful PTL Television Network. She is a woman some have called outrageous and others have called "real life." Whatever her reputation, almost everyone agrees that Tammy is one of the most colorful personalities on Christian television.

What does Tammy think of the constant attention? Downplaying it all, she repeatedly says, "I'm just who I am. With me, what you see is what you get."

A Grandmother's Faith

What you get is Tammy LaValley, the eldest of eight children born to Rachel LaValley of International Falls, Minnesota. As the first in a long line of children, Tammy became the family baby-sitter to Donny, Larry, Judy, Danny, Johnny, Debbie and Ruth. Tammy and Donny shared the same father, while the rest of the children came from a second marriage of Tammy's mother to Fred Grover. It was her stepfather, Fred Grover, whom Tammy called "Daddy," a "wonderful man whom I love dearly," she was to write in her autobiography, *I Gotta Be Me*.

Tammy's parents divorced when Tammy was just three years old. She harbored such bitterness against her father that she refused to see him again for twenty years. "I remember it like it was yesterday. My mother screaming and my father threatening," she says sadly.

Divorce changed life for Tammy and her family. For one thing, her mother's church, the Assemblies of God, would not permit her, as a divorced person, to hold a position in the church or play an instrument. "My mother is a fabulous piano player. There were times when there wouldn't be a pianist at church . . . and they would not let her play because of her divorce. That hurt me. That was one of the first times where I saw the fallacy of how they weren't living what they were preaching."

Above all else, Tammy remembers her Assembly of God Church as a "can't do church." "You can't do this, you can't do that," they would say. Reflecting on those early days, Tammy comments, "I kind of rebelled against all that, because I realized that these people who were telling me you 'can't do' were the ones who were getting into sexual sins, or getting each other's husbands and wives. The people who were more liberal, who were more in touch with themselves and Jesus . . . those were the ones that were finding life so happy that they didn't have to do all those things . . ."

If her church didn't provide Tammy with a strong childhood faith, her Grandmother Fairchild did. "She was the most influential person in my life," Tammy says of her grandmother. "She loved people and she loved Jesus. I can still hear her today, praising the Lord and talking to Jesus. She lived the life she talked about. Through my grandma, I knew salvation and the possibility of living for the Lord."

The faith Tammy's grandmother gave her provided more than just a belief for the hereafter. It was a faith with a "can-do" attitude. "Grandma always used to say, 'Don't you give up, you pick yourself up by your bootstraps. Don't you dare give up!'" Little did Tammy realize what the future held, and the many times her husband, Jim, and PTL would need her grandmother's bootstrap faith.

> *My favorite verse is Romans 8:28. I live it, I eat it, I sleep it. It goes: "For we know that all things work together for good for those that love the Lord, and for those who are called according to His purpose."*
>
> TAMMY BAKKER

SHOW BUSINESS AT SIX

While Tammy's family enjoyed plenty of heaven, they were not overly blessed with this world's goods. In a word, they were poor. The family bathroom was an outside privy; inside, Saturday night was bath night. The cleanest children climbed first into the old galvanized tub filled with hot water from the nearby stove.

Had it not been for her Aunt Gin (for "Virginia"), Tammy probably would never have visited a restaurant or had the opportunity to wear dress-up clothes. It seemed there was never enough money for eight children. With a few extra dollars, Aunt Gin taught Tammy to be a lady, buying her fancy dresses and fixing her hair. In a new dress, Aunt Gin would then take Tammy with her to the Mission Covenant Church. By the age of ten, Tammy considered herself too proper to go to a Pentecostal church like her parents. She refused—that is, until a friend invited her.

Tammy still held resentment toward her Assembly of God Church because of the church's treatment of her mother. "I couldn't understand how they could take her money but wouldn't let her play the piano," she would write later. Nevertheless, Tammy attended a prayer meeting with her friend and "it changed my life." She responded to the preacher's call for repentance and, for hours, stayed near the church altar seeking God. Eventually her mother was summoned to come and take her home.

From that day on, Tammy attended the Assembly of God Church with her family. She recalls those days as "wonderful old-fashioned Pentecostal services." Outside the church, however, it wasn't so easy. Pentecostals like Tammy were called "Holy Rollers" and were subject to ridicule by the outside community.

Things weren't perfect inside the church either. There was a power struggle within the church leadership, and twice the church closed its doors. Her mother was the subject of unkind rumors, rumors that hurt Tammy as well. But Rachel LaValley Grover turned the other cheek more than once. She invited church members into her home and played the role of unofficial hostess to the traveling evangelists who visited the church and its congregation.

It was when one of those traveling evangelistic groups, the A. A. Allen Evangelistic Crusade, came to town that Tammy began to sing in public. She was just six years old and so small she would stand on a chair in front of the microphone, singing her heart out at the tent meetings.

Tammy's discovery of her "show-biz" side formed the

next step toward the making of a Christian TV personality some twenty years later. At age twelve she sang in the school choir and was selected for a part in the musical *Oklahoma!*. From her Sunday school classes, she had learned that "play-acting" was wrong, but Tammy didn't care. It was one of the first times Tammy decided to experiment beyond the boundaries of her "can't do church."

Today, show business is a part of Tammy's everyday life. Her television presence on the PTL Television Network is so important, one close friend says, that Jim Bakker "thinks it's his secret weapon." Laura Lee, wife of singer and PTL regular Doug Oldham, says, "Tammy's the one ingredient they have to have. She's the person who captivates and intrigues people. She's the laughter, the 'movie star,' she's the exciting somebody that they all want to see."

One reason Tammy has such a strong following, particularly among women, is "because she's bold." Bobbie Garn, the director of "Tammy's House Party," says, "Tammy is the voice that will say anything. She does what every woman would like to do and she tries to encourage them to do it and to be whatever they want to be."

> *You don't have to be dowdy to be a Christian. I have had more women tell me, "Tammy . . . I am set free in Jesus because you weren't afraid to stand up for what you thought was right and wear your makeup and wear your wigs and wear your nice clothes."*
>
> TAMMY BAKKER

Part of PTL's success comes from people who tune in just to see what Tammy is going to wear that day, while others say Tammy has "a way of growing on you. You just want to see what she'll do next." Neil Eskelin, a public relations executive at Heritage USA, explains the PTL formula as "a soap opera that is alive. You're watching a daily episode in the lives of Jim and Tammy Bakker. The audience gets to know them intimately."

Tammy's on-camera success hasn't come without criticism, however. What's the number one topic of concern? Her makeup. With her makeup being a perennial concern of the critics, Tammy has developed a simple yet characteristic response, "I don't care." She explains it this way: "I tell them, 'I don't care as long as I'm not offending God.' I want to do as much with myself as I can and it's not for them, it's for my husband. I have the right to do that if I want to."

Not from Kissing

The first time Tammy wore makeup was in the school musical *Oklahoma!* when she was twelve. She felt it made her look prettier, and when she looked prettier, she had more confidence. It was her belief that if acting, or wearing makeup, or even going to the movies was wrong, then God would let her know. She later said, "I discovered that God was more open than I had realized."

Along with the makeup and the acting came boys, a subject she was too embarrassed to discuss with her mother. Still, there were certain questions Tammy had to have answered. One was whether or not you could become pregnant from kissing. When her mother reassured her with, "No, honey, you can't get pregnant from just a boy kissing you," Tammy was relieved. Yet, still she vowed never to let a boy get near her again.

It was a vow Tammy would find hard to keep. For two years in a row Tammy was elected Queen of her summer Bible camp, and boys began to call. When Tammy started dating, her mother laid down strict rules, including curfews. Tammy was allowed to date anyone who was a gentleman, and that included the school "hunk," a young man named Ron. Ron remained the first and only non-Christian that Tammy dated; they went together for two years. When Tammy stopped seeing him in favor of the pastor's son, Ron stood outside Tammy's house in the rain, calling her name.

Ken Johnson was the pastor's son who took Ron's place. Ken had an eye for the girls, but it was Tammy he liked best. At the time, Tammy was working full time at the local Woolworth's store, a job her Aunt Gin helped her get when she was fifteen. After she and Ken graduated from high school, Ken proposed to her. Tammy was elated; not only would she be marrying a pastor's son, but one who wanted to follow in his father's ministerial footsteps. Yet problems soon arose. Tammy also wanted to serve the Lord, but Ken wouldn't hear of it.

Tammy's problems with Ken were more than his wanting a stay-at-home wife. "I believe when a man makes up his mind to marry a woman, the flirting should stop," she says. Both Ken and another boy she was engaged to, Stanley, had problems being one-woman men, so in time Tammy broke off each of the relationships. As she explained later, these early relationships failed for one simple reason: "God wanted me to marry Jim Bakker."

> *On our third date, Jim asked me to marry him and I was shocked. I mean nobody asks you on a third date to marry them, but still, in another way, I knew that he was the right one for me.*
>
> TAMMY BAKKER

REDHEAD, BLONDE, OR BRUNETTE

With some help from Aunt Gin, Tammy enrolled in the North Central Bible College in Minneapolis, Minnesota. "We had an outdoor bathroom all my life, and I had never seen a tall building. I had never seen an ocean, and I had never seen a mountain," Tammy says. Neither had she ever seen anyone quite like Jim Bakker.

When eighteen-year old Tammy LaValley first met the Bakker family, she was convinced they were rich. Their house had two bathrooms and a baby grand piano. It all seemed a long way from Tammy's outside privy and the old galvanized tub. Regardless of the differences between them, soon Jim and Tammy were "totally in love" and began plans to get married. One complication, however, blocked their path—Jim and Tammy's college did not allow students to marry and remain in school. For the elder Bakkers this was a serious problem, for they were strongly against Jim dropping out of school. Tammy and Jim faced a choice between school and each other.

They chose each other.

At the time of their marriage, Jim worked at Rothschild's Restaurant for a woman named Lena, "a wild lady who smoked long cigarettes." Lena soon took the young Bakkers under her wing. When Tammy chose a red dress for her wedding, Lena quickly replaced it with mint-green. She even provided the couple with a wedding cake for their small service. The year was 1961.

To start their new life, Jim and Tammy took a small apartment near the school and decorated it in "Early Salvation Army." Tammy calls those early years the best of times, "the times when we were struggling to make it. They were the times when I did all my own housework and had dinner ready for Jim when he came home every night." Most of all, for Tammy, they were good times because Jim and she were the closest to each other. "Now," she says, "everything is so big, so huge."

Perhaps part of the joy was generated from the sheer excitement of a husband and a new home. Today when she speaks of marriage Tammy says, "The key is to keep it exciting. I like to be different people for my husband. I wear different wigs all the time. Jim never knows if I'm going to be a redhead, a blonde or a brunette. I like to keep him guessing."

I don't care how old you get, I think a woman ought to stay sexy for her husband. She ought to dress sexy and keep herself exciting. I still flirt a lot with my husband at home.

TAMMY BAKKER

Another key to marriage is "not to make a big deal about things that aren't big deals." At a PTL marriage workshop, the Bakkers learned how to "fight fair." Fighting fair, as she explains it, is saying "I" a lot. "You say *I* feel this, *I* feel that, and not, *you* did this, *you* did that. Don't blame the other person and say, you did, you think, you said. Don't tell them what they think . . . it's unfair; you don't know what they're thinking. Fighting fair is saying . . . maybe this is how it is or . . . I'm hurt." After recently celebrating their twenty-fifth wedding anniversary, Tammy feels divorce is just too easy. She continues to preach that to build a successful marriage, you have to work at it—and work hard.

For the first few weeks of their marriage, Jim refused to attend church because he resented the church for denying him and Tammy the opportunity to stay in school and still be together. Tammy was devastated. "I thought, 'What am I going to do? Have I made a mistake?' " While Jim stayed home, Tammy was attending church regularly, even leading the song service at times.

One day Jim received a phone call that persuaded him to return to church. A concerned church member told Jim that "if you don't get back to church and do what God wants you to do, your wife is going to be the minister." That was all the encouragement Jim needed. He wasn't about to be left behind.

I don't think people realize that Jim is really a fabulous preacher. He's one of the best preachers in the country.

TAMMY BAKKER

ON THE ROAD

With Jim again thoroughly committed to his faith, the Bakkers were ready to begin the ministry to which they felt called. Their first mission field was not going to be Minnesota, though. Jim and Tammy had visions of faraway places —they wanted to go to work in the Amazon. Inspired by a visiting missionary, the young Bakkers set out to raise the necessary money by taking their Amazon message on the road.

Their first stop was North Carolina where the Reverend Aubrey Sara invited the Bakkers to hold a revival meeting at his church. At the time, "numbers" were the standard by which revival rallies were judged; everyone hoped to see the altars lined with new decisions of faith. By this standard, Jim and Tammy almost failed before they began. The first few nights of their revival attracted only a muffled response from their listeners and few changed lives. Finally, on the last night, ten people came forward to be baptized. Although the numbers were small, the Bakkers' ministry success had begun.

The couple spent the next few months traveling as a Gospel team, sharing lodging with host pastors and accepting whatever offerings the church could afford. However, their dream of becoming missionaries in South America vanished as quickly as it formed. The missionary who had first inspired the idea, and had agreed to sponsor their ministry overseas, proved himself a phony. It was back to the road for the Bakkers.

Like so many other traveling evangelists of the time, Jim and Tammy opted for the convenience of a house trailer for their life on the road. Their first trailer lasted one day. The manufacturer had failed to weld a seam, and the trailer—dislodged from the car—passed the Bakkers on a four-lane highway. Fortunately, no one was hurt when the trailer crashed and came to rest against a telephone pole. Because the accident could be traced to the faulty weld, the manufacturer compensated the Bakkers with a newer, more expensive trailer at no charge. That second trailer was home for the next five years that the Bakkers spent as traveling ministers.

PUPPETS AT CBN

Oral Roberts had his Gospel tents, Rex Humbard his Humbard Family Singers, and Robert Schuller his drive-in congregation. The Bakkers, too, were seeking a niche, a void to fill with their special talents. They soon found it on top of a Soakie Bubble Bath bottle.

Traveling from church to church, Jim and Tammy discovered that little children sought a strong faith as earnestly as their parents. This was Jim and Tammy's inspiration. They decided to start a children's puppet ministry by using tops from bottles of Soakie Bubble Bath. With a wide variety of animal shapes available to them, they soon made "Susie Moppet" and "Allie Alligator" part of the Bakker ministry. In time, the Bakkers' puppets became so popular that they were featured on prime-time network television—even if the show was "Dick Clark's Bleeps and Blunders." The blunder featured Tammy on "The Jim Bakker Show" with one of the puppet's eyes falling out and rolling across the stage.

With this fresh approach to reaching children, word of the Bakkers' puppets spread quickly. Attendance at their meetings doubled and tripled, with children dragging their parents to church instead of vice versa. Jim and Tammy were soon breaking Sunday school attendance records across the country. It was during one such meeting that the Bakkers were spotted by Bill Garthwaite, a producer with the Christian Broadcasting Network. Garthwaite felt the Bakkers' ministry to children would be perfect for Pat Robertson's then fledgling television network.

Tammy, however, was terrified of being on television, and spent the night before her TV debut crying. "I was out of my mind with total fear," she says. "Even though you're afraid, you just keep doing it. I think the only way you get over fear of anything is just to make yourself do it."

*People think I turn on the waterworks for Jim all the time.
The only time I ever cry is when . . . I'm talking about
the Lord. When I talk about Jesus, I cry because I love
Him so much and He's done so much for me.*

TAMMY BAKKER

While Tammy was trembling, Jim's excitement was growing. He seemed to be a natural in front of the camera, and the new show proved to be a success. Yet this first attempt at broadcasting was just the beginning, for Jim Bakker had big ideas when it came to television. He saw the potential of reaching hundreds of thousands of people with a TV ministry, and he saw the chance of doing that on CBN. When Pat Robertson asked him to do a program for children, Jim jumped at the chance to join CBN full time. The Bakkers canceled a year of revival meetings and moved to Portsmouth, Virginia.

Tammy soon warmed up to the idea of television, especially when the fan mail started to come in. "The Jim and Tammy Show" became the biggest thing ever to hit Christian television. Its setting included a house with a treasure chest full of ten- and fifteen-cent toys. Neighborhood children were rounded up to appear on camera and to serve as the audience. Before long, "The Jim and Tammy Show" could be seen nationwide. Thousands of children joined The Jim and Tammy Club and received friendship rings and decoders through the mail.

At the time, CBN was having financial problems. When no one took the lead, Jim decided to tackle the problem head-on and raise the money himself. "They (CBN) didn't want to admit they had a problem. But Jim said, unless you admit you have a problem, nobody will help you. Jim just broke down and admitted one night on television that CBN was going to go under unless the people gave and God intervened."

Jim Bakker began committing all his waking hours to the CBN network. Many days he would work from six in the morning until one or two the next morning. At the same time, Tammy was hoping for a child. The two had been married now for seven years, and Tammy felt the time was right. Unfortunately, Jim felt they were too busy "working for the Lord" to have children.

"THE 700 CLUB"

Occasionally, the rigorous demands of television broadcasting created havoc within the Bakker marriage. According to Tammy, "the biggest disagreement in our marriage would be how hard Jim works. He works too hard and I feel . . . I'm always fighting for him to spend time with our family and time with me." At one point Tammy felt the ministry had become the "other woman" in their relationship. "I was never jealous," she explains, "just hurt. Jim and I had spent so many years just the two of us together, and we had worked together all the time. All of a sudden, our closeness was leaving. I just felt neglected—left out— like I wasn't needed anymore."

The pressures at CBN eventually took their toll on Jim Bakker. He developed ulcers and shortly after, his nerves were stretched to the breaking point. It was a time of despair for Tammy. "There was a time when Jim couldn't even take a shower because he couldn't stand the water on his body—it felt like needles going through him. And that was a hard time on me too, because I had to do the 'Jim and Tammy Show' by myself. I really thought Jim might never work again."

> *I feel that we've probably come as close to hell as you can come, but God was there and we made it.*
>
> TAMMY BAKKER

One day when Tammy was taking a glass of milk to Jim she dropped the glass, spilling milk all over the hardwood floors. It was a small accident, but it became a moment of anguish for Tammy. "I dropped it and broke it. I didn't know there could be so much milk in a glass. I got down in that milk and just started crying. And the Lord spoke to me and said, 'Tammy, be glad that you have milk to spill and be thankful that you have a husband to take it to.' I never complained after that."

A few weeks later, someone from the ministry sent Jim a book, *Hope and Health for Your Nerves*. Jim read and reread that book until he knew it by heart. Slowly Jim, and also Tammy, began to recover. They watched their diets and started to take better care of themselves physically. Jim was on the mend. Within a month he was back on the old schedule hosting the evening talk show he had originated. That show—"The 700 Club"—was now the flagship program of the Christian Broadcasting Network.

Another despairing time was Jim and Tammy's firing at CBN. One night Jim received a call from the radio show asking him to work the late shift. He refused. The next day he and Tammy were fired. The Bakkers' hard work seemed to be unraveling, but Pat Robertson, the head of CBN, refused to go along with the firing and asked the Bakkers to come back. At that time Jim Bakker was CBN's main fund raiser and Pat could ill afford to lose him. Pat also had a special liking for the Bakkers, inviting them out and helping them with their first home.

TAMMY'S TOUGH TIMES

Both Jim and Tammy enjoyed decorating their new home and in doing so, the subject of a nursery came up. This time, surprisingly, Jim said, "Yes, let's have a baby." A year later, in 1970, Tammy Sue was born.

Tammy called her pregnancy the "greatest thing in the world." Television viewers responded with cards and gifts, including one hundred pairs of booties and enough clothes to last until Tammy Sue's second birthday. Less than a month after the birth of her first child, Tammy returned to work. To help out, Tammy's Grandma Fairchild moved in while Tammy adapted to her new role as mother.

But something was wrong. Sometimes Tammy would cry for no reason at all, and then for days on end she couldn't laugh *or* cry. "It was getting so bad that Jim thought I hated him . . . but I didn't want anybody touching me, I didn't want anybody around me. I was just so depressed all the time." Her doctor dismissed her condition as postnatal depression. It wasn't until later that Tammy learned she had been given an almost fatal dose of medication.

After nine or ten months of turmoil, Tammy was so desperate that she decided to turn to a psychiatrist. She continues the story, "Just as I picked up the telephone book and got the psychiatrist's name, the Lord spoke to me and said, 'Tammy, let Me be your psychiatrist.'"

A few weeks later Tammy received an invitation to sing at a convention. She hadn't sung in months, yet something told her to say yes. It was while singing a Gospel favorite, "The King Is Coming," that she felt healed for the first time. "God delivered me, totally delivered me," says Tammy. "People back in the audience, they literally saw it. It was like Fourth of July sparklers coming up over my head and going down over my whole body. They rose to their feet . . . as the power of the Lord went through that audience and set me free, right there in front of thousands of people."

Today, Tammy's remedy for stress is a little less dramatic —she goes shopping. "I love the walking of it, the exercise of it. And you know what happens? When I'm shopping, I don't think about the bills at PTL, I don't think about anything else. It's just the only time, probably ever, that I get my mind off PTL and the problems and frustrations of running such a huge corporation. There's times I just have to quit thinking and the only way I can quit thinking is by shopping."

I always say shopping is cheaper than a psychiatrist.
With me if I didn't have that time, I probably could not
live.

TAMMY BAKKER

What does Tammy buy when she's out? That's not the point at all. Tammy doesn't like *buying* so much as she likes *shopping.* If you have yet to make this discovery, according to Tammy there is a difference. "The very first place I go is to the sale counter. And very seldom do I ever spend a lot of money on clothes. I like fun things, and fun things aren't real expensive. Another thing I buy is separates, so I can put them together. Then people get the idea that I've got a whole lot more than I really have."

Besides buying shoes—a habit she calls one of her secret "sins"—Tammy craves cubic zirconiums. "You can buy a cubic zirconium for thirty bucks and nobody knows," says Tammy. "Who is going to know and who dares ask you? Any woman can look like she's really got a lot on the ball by buying herself a thirty-dollar cubic zirconium, about three or four carats. People always think all my stuff is real. They would be shocked if they knew what I had, but I'm not going to tell them because it's none of their business."

PTL Is Launched

After eight years of hard work, the Bakkers felt they had gone as far as they could go at CBN. Pat Robertson considered them an important part of the CBN family, yet jealousies continued to stir among the staff. Jim and Tammy talked of leaving but had little intention of doing so. Then in 1972, Jim sensed that God was urging him to resign. That night the Bakkers put their house up for sale; the next day it sold. The CBN chapter in their lives was over.

For a while, the Bakkers traveled from TV station to TV station, hosting telethons and raising money. They had no concrete plans and literally lived on faith, day after day, week after week. Again, they bought a house trailer, using it to tour the country while helping Christian television stations raise funds.

In California, Jim and Tammy met with Paul and Jan Crouch, a couple who hosted a Christian show on cable television. Together, the Bakkers and the Crouches launched the Trinity Broadcasting System with plans to go on the air with a new show. They called it the PTL Club.

On the advice of a close friend from CBN, the two couples formed a corporation with Jim as president. Paul became the business manager, handling the business side of Trinity and PTL, while Jim ran the ministry. For a time the partnership held strong, yet within two years the California dream also came to an end. Business conflicts drove away the Bakkers and twenty-five staff members. The Crouches stayed behind to pick up the pieces and in time built Trinity Broadcasting into one of the nation's leading Christian television networks.

Within a month of their departure, the Bakkers formed another corporation, Dove Broadcasting. They set up offices in the home of a staff member and sent letters to the PTL mailing list. Plans were drawn for a television station, and money started to come in.

Jim and Tammy had now been intimately involved in two Christian television networks. Jim had originated the Christian talk show with "The 700 Club" and was ready to call his own shots. He felt his calling was to be a Christian talk show host.

The next step toward Jim's goal came in 1974 when Jim and Tammy received an invitation to host a telethon in Charlotte, North Carolina. The plan called for just one meeting. That one meeting became a critical turning point, for it established Charlotte as the Bakkers' new home base. In time that home base would include land on the North Carolina–South Carolina border, and would become the site of the multimillion-dollar Heritage USA. It would also be the new home of PTL.

The PTL Television Network began with a two-hour daily program broadcast from a Charlotte furniture store. With the help of a half-dozen workers, the Bakkers built a television studio and started to expand their ministry. They bought time on other stations and were soon broadcasting in twenty separate geographical areas known as television markets.

We are helping people en masse. And that's why we're here. We wouldn't be on television if we couldn't tell people, "Hey, you can make it. Don't give up."

TAMMY BAKKER

Almost immediately, the couple found themselves up against money problems again. Bills weren't being paid, forcing Jim to ask for help on the air. For a while, he took over the financial management of the business until it became too demanding for one person. Yet, as almost all evangelists and their wives can attest, Jim and Tammy would not give up. In four years, the PTL team made the leap from twenty markets to two hundred and fifty. The daily PTL Club aired on more than two hundred television stations and one hundred and twenty-five cable stations. With a viewing audience of more than twenty-five million, PTL became one of the world's largest Christian television networks.

Next came the PTL Satellite Network. In April 1978, it began beaming twenty-four hours of Christian programming daily to all of North America. The satellite network featured a variety of top Christian programs produced by both PTL and other ministries, including a prime-time lineup with Jerry Falwell, Rex Humbard, Oral Roberts, and Robert Schuller.

Today, Tammy can be seen daily on "The Jim Bakker Program" and her own show, "Tammy's House Party." Bobbie Garn, the director of the "House Party," says Jim's show is more spiritual while Tammy's is more fun. According to Bobbie, Tammy most enjoys doing shows about the human body, either on health topics or fashion. "She's a real believer in doing everything you can to make yourself feel good and look good. She's just really intrigued with how your body works . . . second to that, she likes topics on makeup and fashion."

For Bobbie, the show is usually a joy to direct because "Tammy's such a pro. She never stops thinking," says Bobbie. "We always have more than one guest, and if one starts to slack off, she can turn to another person. The fact is that she's so inquisitive. She's always wanting to know more." A second help is that the staff never makes "mistakes" on "Tammy's House Party." There are almost no blunders on Tammy's show, and that's because on "Tammy's House Party" they're ready for most anything—goofs included. Bobbie goes so far to suggest that the "House Party" has a bit of the old Gong Show in it.

An example is the broadcast with a ninety-seven-year-old woman and her recipe for homemade noodles. According to Bobbie "they didn't turn out at all. They tasted like cardboard, and every time the lady would try to pick them up, they would just drop. But this little old lady was sticking with it. It was just hilarious! Tammy had tears coming out of her eyes, she was laughing so hard. That's probably the worst 'mistake' we've had on the show."

In 1976, PTL undertook its most ambitious project—a 1,800-acre Twenty-first Century Christian Retreat Center called Heritage USA. Heritage USA would be located just south of Charlotte, on the North Carolina–South Carolina border. Early plans for the center included the world's largest campground, a family Bible conference and vacation center, a retirement community (renamed a "refirement" community, for senior citizens "refired" about their faith), new studios and a developing educational program for evangelism and communications.

No sooner had the dream begun to take shape than PTL faced its most serious crisis. During the summer of 1978, cash-flow problems began to develop. Construction stopped. In eighteen months, PTL had nearly tripled the size of its staff, from three hundred to eight hundred. According to IBM, the PTL ministry was expanding at a rate of 7,000 percent, and the giving could not keep up with the spending.

During those tough times, criticism was heaped on the ministry on an almost daily basis. The local newspaper, the Charlotte *Observer*, seemed to have a personal vendetta against PTL, exposing the Bakkers' so-called opulent lifestyle and demanding an accounting of personal finances. Based on that story, the Federal Communications Commission began an investigation alleging misappropriation of funds.

Meanwhile Jim took to the airwaves to explain the crisis to viewers. He accepted blame for many of the problems, agreeing that PTL had been somewhat ineffective in managing its funds. He also acknowledged that PTL had embarked on too many projects and had indeed become overextended. Many supporters, however, said that Jim's position was no different than that of hundreds of other businessmen. With the support of thousands of "PTL Partners" and improved management, Jim and Tammy overcame their adversities and were able to keep Heritage USA on track.

> *Whenever Jim gets down, I preach to him. I say, don't give up. God can do anything. I bet I've said it a million times to my husband, no, you're not going to give up. Jim says he wouldn't be in Christian television today if it wasn't for me making him stay in it.*
>
> TAMMY BAKKER

A CHRISTMAS GIFT

Tammy Sue was six years old when Tammy Faye decided it was time to have another child. Tammy's pregnancy with

Jamie Charles was announced on national television, and viewers demanded weekly updates on his development. A few days before Christmas 1976, Jamie arrived and PTL viewers responded with showers of cards and gifts.

Tammy was excited to have a baby in the house for a second time. With a newborn, she was also anxious to emphasize a sense of family again, and that meant more time with Jim. "I love the times with the children. The most wonderful times are when we all have supper together. That's one thing Jim has tried to do for us, to eat with us every night," Tammy says. "I think the closest and the most fun times are when we are a family, the four of us together."

Within a year, old problems began to resurface. Jim again spent endless hours at the Heritage work site, where construction had resumed. Tammy desperately needed some privacy, some time alone with Jim. To get away, they headed west for a vacation. That's when it happened: they decided to separate. And it occurred in, of all places, Hawaii, a lovers' paradise. "I had moved into an apartment right next door to . . . Palmdale Hospital. Jim had asked me to do that when we parted on the beach at Waikiki. He said, 'Please, if you're going to get an apartment, get it next to the hospital. That way, at least there'll be people there who love you.' "

It was a difficult time for Tammy. She had lost her self-esteem. She recalls it as a time when "I was angry at God, I was angry at PTL, I was angry at everyone. Jim had been building so long and I had been hurt so much and felt neglected for so long that I couldn't take it anymore. I thought nobody needed me, nobody wanted me. I was lonely . . . hurting all the time." Quite by coincidence, one of the Palmdale doctors called Tammy one day and asked her to come by the hospital. Tammy had considered getting a job there, so she made an appointment to see him.

"I always wanted to be a nurse, so when he called me over to the hospital, I was glad to go." As it turned out, the doctor was a psychiatrist who administered an I.Q. test to

Tammy. "He told me that I had an extremely high I.Q., and he added that he had suspected such. All of a sudden, I realized I wasn't dumb. I realized that I was an intelligent person, that I was worthwhile. For the first time in my life I had confidence. From that point on, it changed my life."

After several weeks of separation, Jim and Tammy were reconciled. Tammy says that God told her to return to Jim and to "be the wife that I should be." They discussed their problems openly on PTL with viewers applauding their candor. From their trial separation came a singles' ministry at PTL, one of the most successful in the country. "The reason we feel so strongly about single people is because we went through that . . . we hurt and we were lonely. We also have marriage seminars, because we got back together and we want others to have that opportunity."

By 1980 most of the controversy surrounding PTL ended and Tammy was singing on PTL and hosting "The Tammy Faye Show." She is a woman who has to stay busy. "I can't stand not to do something. Even if I had not married Jim, I would have been a Country Western singer or something. But I married Jim knowing that we were going to go forward and win the world for Jesus. And that's what we've set out to do."

TAMMY AND PTL TODAY

It is now 1987 and Heritage USA is a big success. Every day the PTL Television Network enjoys an international audience of fifteen to twenty million people.

Part of PTL's attraction, says Tammy, has been her and Jim's opposite personalities. "I think part of our success is because Jim is more steady and more solid. He's kind of the straight man, and I'm kind of his funny little person. I'm a communicator. I just enjoy people, I enjoy fun, I enjoy laughter." Her outgoing personality also has helped the couple face the criticism of the last twelve years. "It's probably the hardest thing," she admits freely. "I'm always saying, 'Oh, come on, lighten up, Jim. Don't get too serious about yourself. Don't take what the papers say too seriously.' I've always solved things with laughter."

Their personal, down-to-earth style of ministry attracts more than its expected share of fans. According to Neil Eskelin, "the transparency of Tammy Bakker and Jim Bakker comes through in the long run as extremely sincere. If they were not sincere, then the viewers wouldn't have stayed with them for the past decade on television." Tammy puts it more simply: "Jim and I, we have such tender hearts, and we really care. We tell people, 'God worked our marriage out. He can do it for you.' "

As viewers know, Tammy has strong opinions on most current issues, particularly those affecting women and the family. Her outspokenness includes such controversial topics as abortion. "I'm totally against abortion," says Tammy. "Jim and I planned exactly when we were going to have both babies. There's enough birth control around so that there is no reason in the world for a woman to get pregnant that doesn't want to get pregnant. I think if a man and a woman know that they can't raise five children, then they shouldn't have five children. Don't just do it to be doing it, and have all these kids."

Then there is divorce. Even though Tammy's mother divorced, Tammy is firmly against the practice. "I don't think it's right, although my mother was divorced. My father left my mother and would not come back to her. If that happens, there's nothing you can do. I believe God wants us to stay married. I would never want to start over again."

And finally there are Tammy's ideas on how to raise children in the 1980s. "Oh, I don't know," says Tammy. "I used to think I knew how to raise kids. Now, I'm not sure. In teenage years, what I've found with my daughter is . . . being there when she wants to talk and letting her know that I've gone through all the emotions she does. With little kids like Jamie . . . the most important thing is being there at night time and just doing lots of hugging and lots of kissing."

Tammy also emphasizes the importance of keeping lines of communication open between her children and herself. Some subjects, however, she finds difficult to discuss. "Sex is always the hardest thing. Once you get free from the scariness of it, then it's not hard anymore . . ."

For all her independence, Tammy still believes that the man should be the head of the house. "I think one of the most important things in the world is to allow a man to be a man, to feel like a man. Don't ever tell him, 'That's a stupid idea.' Don't bring him down. Be supportive of him, encourage him. I believe in keeping the male ego intact."

And what of women's liberation? "I think Christian women are the most liberated women in the whole world," she insists. "I love being under submission to my husband. I love having my husband to lean on. That, to me, is not a lack of liberation." Yet, Tammy still believes that a woman should be her own person, even when it comes to motherhood and work. "I say if a woman wants to work, let her do it. If she wants to stay home and be a housewife, do that. But she shouldn't be home and be a housewife . . . and hating her children for keeping her there."

In her own career, Tammy considers it her task to shake up Christian television. "Christian television is basically very boring. You get those little trios up there that can't sing. You just want to die. And so many of these preachers get on and they preach and preach, just the same old thing. I feel part of my calling is to keep it a little bit interesting, at least."

Keeping it interesting, however, doesn't mean shaking the audience with politics. Tammy has definitely decided to leave that arena to others. "You're damned if you do and you're damned if you don't," says Tammy. "It's a no-win situation. If you're a Republican, the Democrats are mad at you. If you're a Democrat, then the Republicans are mad at you. We have to minister to all people . . ."

We love the Republicans, we love the Democrats. We love the liberals and the others. We're not here to make a political statement.

TAMMY BAKKER

Tammy's avoidance of politics has not stopped her from developing close friendships with many top political leaders. In fact the opposite has been true. Over the years the Bakkers have played host to President and Mrs. Reagan, former President Carter, and other celebrities including Pat and Shirley Boone, Mickey Rooney, Richard Simmons, and Gavin and Patti McLeod, he of "Love Boat" fame. The McLeods, especially, are among the Bakkers' closest friends.

Despite the fact that Tammy claims so many famous people as close friends, Tammy is not a person who is overawed by fame. "People are people no matter where you go . . . I mean, President Reagan has to brush his teeth too, right?" In many ways Tammy considers herself just one of the working people at PTL. And it's that down-to-earth attitude which she says attracts famous people to her. "That's why I get along well with the movie stars, because I'm not afraid of them . . . I've taken some of the biggest stars to Woolworth's to eat. I don't treat them any differently than anybody else."

Tammy has often said, "With me, what you see is what you get." And it's true: the private Tammy Bakker is much like the person you see on TV. She's outgoing, always busy, and she follows her own advice, particularly on marriage. She wants to look attractive for her husband so she rarely goes without makeup, even to bed. "Jim has very seldom seen me without makeup and hardly ever in my life without my eyelashes. I think every woman ought to wear eyelashes. Because I think the eyes are such an important part of the face."

Today, Tammy's greatest source of joy is her children, Tammy Sue, now seventeen, and Jamie Charles, eleven.

She thinks that children today grow up too fast and that robs them of their childhood. "It's not easy to try to get them to stay children. They all want to go their own different ways so quickly." Last year, Tammy Sue began singing professionally and recorded her first record. It is being released by a secular distributor. "We never pushed anything on our children. But I'm ready for Tammy Sue to take over some of my ministry."

As for the future, Tammy says, "I just want to be faithful in whatever God has. I don't have any big dreams of what to accomplish." Jim is the dream-maker in the family, and Tammy is content to let him make the plans for the both of them. "His whole philosophy is that unless you're moving forward, you're going backward. He says we'll always be building, always be going on." When Heritage USA is finished, the Bakkers hope to take their dreams to California. "When it reaches capacity here and our land is filled, then we'll go on to another state and do it again."

Above all, Tammy Faye Bakker wants to be remembered as someone who cared. "I just want them to say, well, she was just what she was. She was the same way she was on television. She was an honest, hard-working gal who really cared about other people."

MACEL FALWELL

❦❧

I told Jerry before I married him that I never wanted to marry a preacher. . . . I didn't want to have to do everything, the group leader, the prayer group. . . . When we first got married, I told him I just was not going to be like most preachers' wives.

MACEL FALWELL

Macel Falwell is certainly not like most preachers' wives, but then neither is Tammy Bakker. Both Macel and Tammy have refused to conform to the traditional role of a preacher's wife. However, their ways of nonconforming are worlds apart. One might say their "differing" is quite different.

While Tammy thrives on television and public attention, Macel craves privacy. When asked if she would do a women's TV show for her husband's cable network, with a firm yet gentle Southern accent Macel replied, "No. But I might change my mind. I've just always stayed in the background and liked it that way."

Tammy Bakker is a performer; she enjoys show business and her Hollywood friends. Again, Macel is different. According to the Falwells' older son, Macel's main concern is "Lynchburg, that's her environment." Even when Moral Majority is making front-page news across the country, the response is the same: "What happens locally in Lynchburg is more important than what someone at the Washington *Post* thinks."

Then there's this question: "Who does the pushing in the family, and who gets pushed?" For the Bakkers, it's Tammy; she does much of the pushing. Interestingly enough, it's the same for the Humbards, the Robertses, the Schullers, and the Swaggarts. It's the wives who keep pushing their husbands onward and upward. Yet with Jerry and Macel Falwell the opposite is true: Jerry pushes Macel. It all began during their six years' courtship.

ROUGH EDGES AND A SLOW START

Macel Pate first met Jerry Falwell January 20, 1952. Macel is remarkably candid regarding that first meeting. "I wasn't very impressed," she recalls. "I thought he was nice, but it was not love at first sight, by any means."

Like so many in the ministry, the young couple met at church. Macel was playing the piano at Park Avenue Baptist Church and Jerry "came over one Sunday, because he heard that there were a lot of pretty girls there." Jerry—who was with a close friend named Jim—looked over and said, " 'I'm going to take that one [meaning Macel].' And Jim looked over and said, 'I'll take the other one [referring to Macel's best girlfriend, who was playing the organ].' "

There were two compelling reasons for a young church pianist not to be "very impressed" with a teenage Jerry Falwell. To begin with, Macel was engaged at the time, and not just to anyone, but to a young man who would be Jerry's roommate at college two years later. A stronger detraction was Jerry's background; it simply didn't work in his favor.

Macel's mother remembered Jerry "as a gruff sort, who was not really ill-mannered, but he had a lot of rough edges." As Macel explains, Jerry's "dad drank, and they sort of had a reputation around town as being tough. She

[Macel's mother] didn't want me to go with him. So first I sneaked around." Jerry was not from a "Fundamentalist" Christian home, although on Sunday mornings his mother would tune in to the "Old-Fashioned Revival Hour," broadcast by Charles E. Fuller, one of the pioneers of radio evangelism. It perhaps was that program which later prompted Jerry Falwell to name his own broadcast "The Old Time Gospel Hour."

To this day, Jerry Falwell says of himself, "I'm a street fighter by nature."

In contrast, Macel's family was always in church. "In fact, I don't ever remember a time when we didn't attend." She describes her mother and father as "godly Christians" who practiced what they preached. Her father, in particular, practiced and preached honesty to his four children. "I've never heard him lie in his entire life. He was so honest that if someone at the grocery store gave him too much change, he would walk five miles to take it back."

The differences between Macel and Jerry were significant, yet Jerry Falwell persisted. "He saw my two older sisters unmarried," says Macel, "and he asked if I intended to be like that or if I was going to get married." Jerry eventually did impress Macel, mostly as a man who was a lot like her father. "I always depended on my dad to take care of me . . . and I guess I was looking for someone very much like him." Both Jerry and Macel were eighteen when they met, but it would be six years before they married. "I finally decided that he was the one. I probably would not have married Jerry if he hadn't just *pushed, pushed, pushed.*"

POWER POLITICS

Jerry Falwell has continued to push throughout his career, always with Macel at his side. When he started the Thomas Road Baptist Church, every afternoon he would knock on more than a hundred neighborhood doors to expand the membership. Although he proudly says, "I have always been a pastor at heart," much of America knows him best as a political advocate for conservative causes. What does Macel think of her husband turned politician? Perhaps their older son, Jerry Jr., puts it best: "She's a preacher's wife, that was the idea when they married and that's what she enjoys. . . . She never intended to marry a politician."

To this day, power politics, on an issue-by-issue basis, seem to hold little interest for Macel. Her husband, Jerry, admits, "Macel has never attempted to influence me on political issues. She reads a great deal. She is very knowledgeable about what is happening everywhere. She is able to give me her personal feelings on almost every important issue. But she has never tried to sway my position." Macel explains that Jerry's political activism "doesn't bother me as long as it is a moral issue. Most of them are. I give him my opinion, and if it's really something that he hadn't thought about, he might change a little. If it's something that he feels very strongly about, I might disagree, but he still has his convictions."

> *On one issue of abortion (i.e., rape) I did say something like "Jerry, now think about that if it were your daughter." Then he thought about it in a different way.*
>
> MACEL FALWELL

THE EARLY YEARS

When Jerry and Macel first met, Jerry was a sophomore at Lynchburg College, majoring in mechanical engineering. A top-notch student in high school, he had earned a 98.6 grade point average and also excelled in football, baseball, and basketball. He was slated to give the valedictorian's speech at graduation, but was barred from doing so when school officials discovered he and other athletes had used bogus lunch tickets to receive free meals for a year.

With his conversion to Christianity—it occurred the same night Jerry met Macel at Park Avenue Baptist Church —Jerry decided to transfer to the Baptist Bible College in Springfield, Missouri. At the same time he turned down an offer to play with the St. Louis Cardinals' baseball organization.

While studying in Missouri, Jerry carried on a long-distance courtship with Macel back in Virginia; he also chose the ministry as his life's work. Macel enjoyed the thousand-mile dates, but was disappointed in Jerry's choice for a vocation. "Most of the preachers I had been around really didn't care about their families," says Macel. "I told him then, when he decided to go into the ministry, that I was not very happy about it. . . ." Jerry reassured her, saying, "I don't expect you to do anything that you're not comfortable with."

After graduating from Baptist Bible College, Jerry made plans to move to Macon, Georgia, to start a church; but before he made the move, leaders from Macel's home church asked him to stay in Lynchburg. "The church we were in had a little problem," recalls Macel. "So a group of us left, including most of the deacons. . . . We talked to Jerry because there were just too many good people that were discouraged." With that invitation, Jerry Falwell began his ministry. The year was 1956.

Services that first Sunday in 1956 were held at the Mountain View Elementary School, the school Jerry Falwell had attended as a boy. A week later, the congregation of thirty-five moved to an abandoned building owned by the Donald Duck Bottling Company. For years, community children called that facility "Donald Duck Baptist Church." Its rightful name was the Thomas Road Baptist Church.

Also during those early days—in fact, it was only seven days later—Jerry began a daily half-hour radio broadcast. In another six months he introduced the "Old Time Gospel Hour" on television. With the aid of TV, the fledgling church swelled to 864 members by the anniversary of its first year. Macel remembers, "At first he had one local TV station, and then two, and then it just grew from there."

A WAY WITH MONEY

Two years after Thomas Road Baptist Church was founded, and six years after their first meeting, Macel Pate and Jerry Falwell got married. It was 1958, and Macel was working at a local bank, a job she held for several years. With her practiced understanding of money and banking, Macel took on the task of managing the family finances. The good sense of that decision was obvious, for Jerry's outgoing, generous manner extended to cosigning almost anyone's bank loans.

"Every time we turned around, we were having to pay off somebody's note," says Macel. "He would do anything in the world for anybody." Many of the notes came into the bank where Macel worked. Eventually it became so bad, Macel convinced her boss not to accept Jerry Falwell's signature any longer. To this day, Jerry Falwell doesn't have a checking account and "he cannot write on mine. He's not the least bit concerned about his personal money."

> *He used to give his clothes away all the time . . . he has actually taken his shoes off and given them to people. In the early days, I knew if we were ever going to have food on the table . . . I would have to manage the money. He doesn't know what he makes . . . he doesn't even see his paycheck.*
>
> MACEL FALWELL

The first place Macel helped keep Jerry Falwell on balance was family finances; the second has been with his "*High Noon* personality." As Jerry explains, "I am a street fighter by nature and shoot from the hip quite regularly. Macel has been a tremendous help in holding me back from taking leaps in the dark or making broad statements that would later have adversely affected the ministry." Macel admits that Jerry's tough style often slips out. On such occasions she'll say something like "Oh, Jerry, you're acting the way you used to. Don't do that anymore." Yet "it's helpful to him," continues Macel, "because he sticks to things, and you know he's going to get it done. No obstacle is too large for him."

The Falwells' younger son, Jonathan, has his own thoughts on how his mother has helped his father. "It was probably thirty years ago when she straightened him out. She gives him a lot of advice . . . how to work things . . . and he listens to her." Well, perhaps.

One area in which Macel did help "straighten out" Jerry was public speaking. When he was learning public speaking over thirty years ago, she would critique his messages and provide "very important advice on my enunciation, gestures, and other important components of . . . public speaking." As Jerry says, "From the very beginning of our relationship and throughout our marriage she has been my best critic."

STARTING A FAMILY WITH DR. SPOCK

At almost every turn, Macel was ready to help Jerry with his career; yet for her, marriage and family always came first. Her longtime friend Mrs. Shirley Burton says, "There were times when some would say . . . she should take a more active role in the church and travel more with Jerry. Often against some ridicule, she stood her ground."

Macel's enthusiasm for the family waned, however, when it came to children. "I didn't want children because I had never been around children. . . . I didn't particularly like to hear them cry and I didn't like all the unpleasant things about babies."

Over time, preferences have a way of changing, and Macel's preferences against children were no different. After four years of marriage the Falwells were ready to start a family.

One year Macel asked Jerry what he'd like for Christmas and he answered, "Well, I really would like to have a little boy." She soon became pregnant, but she didn't tell her husband for three months; she wanted it to be a Christmas present. When she finally told Jerry, "he cried. He didn't believe it," recalls Macel. "He really *didn't* believe it" until Macel produced the prescription her doctor had given her for morning sickness. "Then he was so excited he told everybody."

When Jerry Jr. was born in 1962, Macel called herself a "baby with a baby." In fact, her doctor was so skeptical, he kept her in the hospital an extra week until she became accustomed to her newborn child. When she returned home, Macel approached motherhood the same way she approaches most everything: with a determination to be perfect. "I read every book that was available, Dr. Spock included. Everything had to be perfect."

A simple example illustrates Macel's uncertainty with children. Because she feared her first child would choke, Jerry Jr. didn't learn to eat solid food until he started school at age five. "I'd never been around children, so I didn't know that you were supposed to feed them solid foods. Once my dad tried to give Jerry Jr. some bread and I said, 'Please don't. He's going to choke.'"

Macel spent the first six weeks of Jerry Jr.'s life at her parents', "because they thought I couldn't take care of the baby, which I couldn't." Macel's father soon urged her to "throw those old books away, then your children would have some sense." Macel was still uncertain.

Jerry didn't read the books, but he did play an important role in raising his children. He "did everything I did. He changed the diapers. He got up with them at night and fed them." During one late night feeding, Macel awoke to check on Jerry and his namesake—and found the two asleep in a rocking chair.

After she'd kept Jerry Jr.'s impending arrival secret, Jerry told Macel, "You can never do that to me again." But do it again she did, this time on Father's Day 1964. Macel had given Jerry a Father's Day card signed " 'Jerry Jr. and baby sister.' I told him how much she was going to weigh, and what her name was going to be." When Jeannie was born, on Macel's father's birthday, she weighed within a few ounces of Macel's guesstimate.

JERRY'S SUCCESSES; MACEL'S DOUBTS

While Macel was building a family, Jerry was building what was to become the nation's second largest church. In 1959, three years before Jerry Jr.'s arrival, Jerry Sr. founded the Elim Home for Alcoholics in memory of his father, who at the age of fifty-five died of alcoholism. This first foundation was followed by:

—Lynchburg Christian Academy, in 1967, a full-time day school;

—Liberty Baptist College, in 1971, renamed Liberty University;

—Liberty Bible Institute, in 1972, a home study program;

—Liberty Baptist Theological Seminary in 1973.

In 1968 the "Old Time Gospel Hour" moved from the local TV studio to the church sanctuary. Three years later the program was broadcast nationwide. At about the same time, membership at the Thomas Road Baptist Church neared ten thousand, while the church became involved in overseas work, sending missionary teams to Haiti, Indochina, and South Korea.

Clearly Jerry Falwell was a success, yet that didn't alter Macel's conservative and sometimes doubting nature. "I remember when he bought Treasure Island Youth Camp [an island on the James River in Lynchburg]. I told him, 'That's so silly, you can never pay for it.' He said, 'You just wait, it's going to be fine.' And it turned out great." She also doubted Jerry's decision to build the Lynchburg Christian Academy and Liberty Baptist College. "I remember saying, 'I'm not going to send my child to a Christian school,' because the ones I knew were inferior. And Jerry responded, 'I wouldn't start it if it wasn't going to be the best.' "

These differences between Jerry and Macel spring in part from their opposite personalities. "I guess you could call me a little pessimistic where Jerry is optimistic all of the time. My dad never believed in going into debt or taking a chance in life. I have a lot of that in me. I want to have everything organized in life, and Jerry is the opposite." Macel freely admits her skeptical nature—she has no reason not to. She feels her doubts have had little effect on her husband's goals. Once "he sets his mind to something . . . he just goes," says Macel. "He's a motivator. He never gets discouraged, in spite of everything."

> *He's always had more faith than I have . . . I guess I think smaller than he does. Back in the earlier days of the church, I thought well, one of these days, we just may have a thousand members. I just never dreamed that it would be anything like it is now.*
>
> MACEL FALWELL

Perhaps Jerry appreciates Macel's questioning mind more than she realizes. When it comes to solving problems, Jerry finds that "Macel is very creative. She always has an alternative to my initial ideas and plans. In most cases she is able to add very important and thought-provoking ideas." And Macel's ideas don't stop with Jerry; they extend to many of the key issues women face today. Her opinions may be different from what some might expect.

"I think women should be equal. Definitely," says Macel. "But I do like men to open the door for me." She also firmly believes that "if I were working, I should have the same opportunity. I should get the same pay for doing the same job." Macel recalls her own frustrations working at a local bank and "training a man to do a job who would make more than I for the same work."

On the subject of working women, Macel believes that the ideal situation is to stay home with a child. "But if you absolutely had to work, then I think you could make it work by spending quality hours with your children."

DECISIONS, DEVOTIONS, AND DOGS

As the Lynchburg church grew in popularity, the demands on Jerry's time increased. Macel in the meantime became both mother and father to Jerry Jr., Jeannie, and Jonathan (born in 1966). Macel's best friend, Shirley Burton, contends that "Jerry could never have accomplished what he did without Macel. Seeing the way their children have turned out, there is no question that she made the right decision."

Macel decided early to safeguard her family's privacy and see that the children had as normal a childhood as possible. Despite Jerry's hectic schedule, "he makes certain that he's available for important occasions in the children's lives. He has never missed one of our birthdays, our anniversary, anything that's important to the children. Jeannie has been taking piano lessons since she was five years old, and he's never missed a recital."

One of the Falwells' early decisions was to establish a family routine. It included daily devotions and nightly phone calls home when Jerry was out of town. "When he had to be gone . . . he made it a point to call, no matter how late it was. I remember once around 2 A.M. Jerry called . . . and I heard Jerry Jr. on the extension say, 'Hi, Daddy.' " When Macel asked, "What are you still doing up?" Jerry Jr. replied, "Well, I was just waiting for Daddy to call."

When Jerry's on the road, Macel usually knows his schedule within a few minutes. "He always lets us know where he is and how to reach him. I can find him within five minutes at any time." With Jerry gone, Macel would then lead the family devotions, which were scheduled every night at eleven o'clock. "We generally read some Scripture, then discuss it and have prayer. If he didn't get home until late, he would go to each of their rooms and pray—every night."

Perhaps the most unexpected habit in the Falwell family routine is their late nights. The entire lot are night owls. "We all stay up late," says Macel. "It's not at all unusual to come to my house and see the lights on at two in the morning." Eventually the Falwell children learned that the best time to talk over personal problems with Mom and Dad was late, sometimes very late, at night.

And then there were the family vacation plans, or lack of plans—the Falwell approach to vacations included almost no routine. For a woman who likes her life organized, Macel seldom planned a family vacation. "What we'd do is get in the car and ask the children, 'Where would you like to go?'" One year one child wanted to go to Niagara Falls and another to California. They ended up doing both.

> When the children were young, Macel decided to accompany Jerry to Israel, but without the children. She says, "I was so miserable . . . I called home so many times, Jerry said, 'Never again. Next time, we're going to take the children, because it's less expensive.'"

As the children grew, Macel remained the ever nervous mother. "Every time I read something in the paper about some child having meningitis or polio, I would call the doctor. I was sure my child had every symptom." Only after the birth of her younger son, Jonathan, did she overcome her inner fear of raising children. In contrast, Jerry was more at ease with the children and more willing to let them make mistakes.

With Jerry being very lenient, it was up to Macel to hand

out the discipline. Son Jonathan explains, "Mom was mainly the disciplinarian . . . Dad's soft. He'll let you get away with anything, but Mom was always the stickler for doing things." Macel agrees. "When they were young, I started training them in the way I wanted them to act when they went to other people's homes. I didn't like for them to pick up things from my coffee table and break them or something. Then, when we went to someone else's home, you never saw them running around or touching things."

While being strict with discipline, Macel learned to handle each child differently, "to give them a sense of their own individuality. . . . We always listen to our children, and they've had a part in everything we've done." When the children were small, Macel thought it would be a good idea for them to have a dog. It seemed an appropriate way to foster responsibility. Jerry wanted to get a dog for each child. "We compromised on two," says Macel. "The two younger children had to share one dog, and Jerry Jr. had his own."

THE PUSH OF THE PRESS

With almost all success comes criticism, and there was no exception for Jerry Falwell. By 1972 Jerry was traveling 250,000 miles a year and his television program was aired on more than 260 stations a week—nearly 350 stations carried his radio program. As his popularity grew, so did the media attention.

According to Jerry Jr., "Over the years . . . Dad's image has changed . . . it's gotten better. At first it was a lot of bad press. A lot of the media covered him to use him as an example of extremism. After a couple of years it became evident that he wasn't as extreme as they had hoped."

What does Macel think of the reporting? Jerry's press coverage is one topic on which Macel has explicit opinions, especially on her husband's tough image.

"I think the press has definitely created it. They always

leave the family out of it. If they come here and say it's going to be a family-type [report], it never is. They like to ignore that he's even married. I don't understand why. . . . What do they get out of it?" Even as Macel asked the question, she realized the answer. It's all rather simple: "If they had to show the family, they'd have to show him as a very loving husband and father, and they don't want to do that."

The absence of that family image is what bothers Macel the most. "I think the greatest misunderstanding is that [people] don't know that he is so human . . . so loving. He's very sensitive to people. They think he's some tough political figure, when he really isn't at all."

Part of the excitement in the Falwell family has been Jerry's prankster personality. "He's always been a joke-ster," says Macel. "Shortly after we were married, Jerry went to Florida and came back with an alligator. I didn't know anything about it. When I went into the bathroom the next morning . . . I heard this 'plop' in the bathtub. I couldn't imagine what it was, and I turned around and there was the alligator . . . as long as the bathtub. I was so shocked, I ran out screaming."

> *The criticism "really hurt in the early days when it first started. It was difficult, and a lot of times I hated to go out. . . . Finally I just learned to deal with it."*
> MACEL FALWELL

While the press continued to hound Jerry, Macel faced her most difficult times when her mother and father died. She calls the death of her mother, of cancer, in 1973 "the worst day I've ever experienced." She remembers that while she was visiting her mother in the hospital, her mother had a vision that Jonathan had been hurt. "She said, 'Macel, go to Jonathan . . . he's bleeding. He's cut all over.' And I told her no, he was okay, but she insisted that I go to him. When I got home, Jerry told me that

Jonathan . . . had had a wreck [an accident] and was bleeding all over."

This was the first time that anyone whom Macel was close to had died. Eleven years later she went through it again with her father, the man who would walk five miles to maintain his integrity. "With a Christian, I think it's much easier," says Macel, "because you know they're in heaven and that you'll see them again one day."

THE GROWING FALWELL MINISTRY

In 1985 Liberty Baptist College was renamed Liberty University. By then the college had become an accredited four-year liberal arts institution offering bachelors degrees in business administration, religion, communications, education, natural science, and other fields. The expanded curriculum was accompanied by a new campus built on Liberty Mountain. Today the 4,700-acre university consists of some forty buildings and an array of TV and radio courses. "Our vision," says Chancellor Dr. Jerry Falwell, "is to soon have all the schools on Liberty Mountain. We want 50,000 young Champions for Christ."

At the same time the Thomas Road Baptist Church continued to expand. In 1970 the church budget was $1 million. By 1985 the budget for the total ministry had soared to $100 million and covered more than two thousand employees. Currently more than $300,000 is spent for weekly air time for the "Old Time Gospel Hour," now carried on some 390 television stations and a nationwide network of radio stations. In addition, Jerry Falwell is involved with the publishing of a nationally circulated newspaper, the *Liberty Report*, and a magazine, *The Fundamentalist Journal*.

The growth of the Jerry Falwell ministries can, for the most part, be attributed to Jerry's movement into the political arena. Throughout the 1960s and early '70s the Rev. Dr. Falwell had purposely avoided using the pulpit as a forum for political issues. In the later 1970s he made an about-face and began his climb into political notoriety. One of the first projects was a tour of "I Love America" rallies. The year was 1976, America's Bicentennial, and the Falwell ministry celebrated by touring 112 major cities with two hundred students from Liberty Baptist College. The goal was simple: to bring America "back to God."

These rallies set the stage for creating the organization for which Jerry Falwell is best known by many—Moral Majority. Founded in 1979, the organization soon propelled Jerry Falwell and his ministry into the limelight.

Acting as a private citizen, Dr. Jerry Falwell recruited a handful of conservative professionals to lobby for such causes as school prayer and anti-abortion legislation. As Jerry said in 1980, "the Moral Majority is pro-life, pro-family, pro-moral . . . and very strongly pro-Jewish and pro-American." Moral Majority became Falwell's first secular enterprise, embracing the same causes as his ministry, but acting separately from the Thomas Road Baptist Church. The name "Moral Majority" was suggested by Paul M. Weyrich, a Roman Catholic who heads the Committee for the Survival of a Free Congress. Weyrich became one of the founding fathers of Moral Majority.

In its earliest stages, Moral Majority concentrated in four areas: education, lobbying, endorsement of candidates, and legal aid. It is in the third area that the organization has shown its strength. That strength was first felt in the elections of 1980. Through door-to-door campaigns, Moral Majority favorites won in such states as Alabama, Alaska, Indiana, Iowa, and Oklahoma.

With his political success, Jerry Falwell again faced strong criticism. At one point the criticism became so strong that the Falwells were receiving two hundred threats each month. It was partly because of these threats that in 1980 the family moved into a large, twelve-room house, purchased by an Atlanta benefactor. The house is situated on six acres and surrounded by an eight-foot cinder-block wall. The only entrance is through a set of electronic gates, manned by a guard. Despite such precautions, the Falwell mailbox has been blown up several times.

> *The only thing that would really upset him is if they said something about the family. Otherwise, he doesn't let things bother him.*
>
> MACEL FALWELL

In late 1986 Jerry Falwell decided to redirect his political activities. He called it the most important decision of his career.

During the seven years since the forming of Moral Majority, Jerry feels he's won many victories for the conservative cause. He writes: "There's a new feeling of pride in America. All the polls indicate that America has moved to the right politically and theologically. Thousands of pastors became, and remain, involved in political, social, and moral issues. The time has come to get back to basics." For pastor and chancellor Jerry Falwell, "getting back to basics" means devoting his remaining years preaching the Gospel and building Liberty University into a world-class university.

According to Jerry Jr., his mother again had doubts. Macel was concerned about how the public might respond. When "Dad recently decided to downplay his political activities, she wasn't sure that it was a good idea. She thought it might be viewed as a retreat." With characteristic firmness, Jerry says no. "For now, I believe God wants me to focus more of my energy on the ministry. But if someone tells you, 'Jerry Falwell is getting out of politics'—don't believe him."

NEVER ON BIRTHDAYS

By 1979 there were three teenagers in the Falwell household. Macel recalls dreading the teenage years, but when they arrived, the children were no different. "One day one of them came to me and said, 'Mama, I just want to apologize to you.' And I asked, 'For what? What have you done?' 'Well, for the way that I acted when I was going through the teenage years. . . .' I was not even aware of any misdeeds."

Macel had her standard "sex education" talk with each child when he or she turned twelve. "I told them, 'I'd rather you come to me and talk about it instead of going to your friends, because if you hear it from your friends, you get the slanted view. . . .'" One son did approach his mother with a question. "He said, 'Mom, you know you told me if I had any questions, to come in and ask you.' I couldn't imagine what it was going to be. I thought I'd covered everything pretty well. He said, 'How do you kiss a girl?' Now, explain that to a son!"

Several years ago, television reporter Rona Barrett did an interview with the Falwells, in which she asked Jeannie, then sixteen, if she would ever have premarital sex. According to Macel, "Jeannie says, 'No, I wouldn't.' Rona then asked, 'Is it because your father wouldn't let you?' And Jeannie answered, 'No, my father wouldn't have anything to say about it if I wanted to do it. I wouldn't do it simply because I don't believe in it, and I wouldn't want to hurt my father.'"

Perhaps the special relationship Macel has with her children can best be illustrated by an event that took place at the home of millionaire Bunker Hunt of Texas. "There was a huge crowd there . . . Mrs. Bob Hope was at our table . . . just about everybody you can imagine. The children had gone with us, but they were seated at another table. While we were listening to Bob Hope, I whispered to Jerry, 'Here we sit with all these famous people and I'd rather be sitting with our children.'"

Jerry's commitment to the children has been equally strong. "We have committed ourselves to a very close family relationship," says Jerry. "The husband who allows anything to come ahead of his wife and children makes a serious mistake." Once Jerry's secretary had mistakenly booked Jerry out of town on the birthday of his youngest son. When Jerry found out, he offered to cancel the meeting or give the honorarium to Jonathan. Jonathan chose to have his father, and Jerry canceled the meeting.

THE FALWELLS TODAY

Jerry and Macel Falwell's homelife has not changed in almost thirty years, an accomplishment for which Macel can take credit. Friend Shirley Burton says, "There is an imaginary line that no one but family can cross. . . . She takes care of her own family and only gets outside help once in a while." Son Jonathan concurs. "The house, the cars, and everything that's done around here with the family, pretty much she takes care of. And that's kind of taken a lot of pressure off of my dad."

To the three Falwell children Jerry is "just like any father would be," says Jonathan. "I don't think he's any different than anyone else." One key difference is that their father created his own university—Liberty University—which in time all three children attended. In 1983 their mother joined them on campus. "Every year, after the children got older, I'd want to go to school . . . and then I would back out." Although Macel was an honor student in high school, she lacked the confidence to go to college.

As he had always done, Jerry encouraged her. In 1983 daughter Jeannie, on orders of her father, enrolled her mother in classes. "I still thought, I don't have to go, even though she's enrolled me." Jerry, however, had other plans. That Sunday, Jerry announced in church his wife was a full-time student. When Macel asked why, he replied, "So you couldn't back out."

Graduation date for Macel and her son Jonathan is May 1987. She is studying English and psychology and may use her degree to write. "If I wanted to get a job, I would go do it. Jerry would not care one bit. In fact, after Jerry Jr. was born, I said I really don't want to work. . . . Still I went back and worked, and then decided I would rather be with my child."

Through the years, Macel feels she has derived her greatest joy from her children. Her only regret is that she didn't "start having children earlier, so I could have enjoyed them longer." Today, with her children building their own separate lives, Macel says she's happy; but, like most mothers, she's not looking forward to the day they leave home permanently. She does, however, look forward to being a grandmother. "I'll be a terrific grandmother," says Macel.

Older son Jerry Jr. is completing law school at the University of Virginia and may represent the ministry as a lawyer. Daughter Jeannie is currently in medical school, and younger son Jonathan will have graduated from Liberty University in the spring of 1987 with a degree in political science. He is the most likely candidate to follow in his father's ministry.

The accomplishments of his father will be a high standard for Jonathan to live up to. Over the years, Jerry Falwell has been honored by Christians and non-Christians alike. In 1979 the Religious Heritage of America named him Clergyman of the Year, and Food for the Hungry International honored him in 1981 as Christian Humanitarian of the Year. *U.S. News & World Report* called him one of the "Most Influential People" in America in 1983, and he has twice been named by a *Good Housekeeping* readers' poll as the second most admired man in the United States.

To what does Macel attribute her husband's success? A large part has been Jerry's street-fighting attitude. For Macel, that tough attitude has turned Jerry into "a motivator. . . . He never gets discouraged." Yet still she continues to wish people could see his caring side more often. "We'll go into a restaurant sometimes and Jerry will hear from a waiter that someone is celebrating a birthday or anniversary or something. And he always picks up the tab."

Along with that motivating attitude has been Macel's

ever watchful eye. "One of my favorite things is people watching," says Macel. "There have been so many times that I have sort of helped him in his relationships with people. He doesn't tend to see the expression on someone's face or something in a room." On those occasions Macel would say, " 'You know, I think you really need to say something to that person.' And he would do it."

In an indirect way, Macel keeps an even closer eye on the ministry's bottom line. That bottom line is not money; it's philosophical. According to Jerry Jr., in some ways his mother is "more fundamental, more conservative than my father. Her ideals have been engrained in her since she was a child. She's the one that kind of keeps Dad true. . . ." All this makes one wonder if Macel is indeed the power behind the Jerry Falwell throne. "A lot of people say that I do fit that role," says Macel. Her older son would most likely concur. When asked if, in an indirect way, he thought his mother had had quite an influence on the country, he firmly responded, "Yes, I would say so."

As Macel and Jerry Falwell face the future and reflect on the past, Macel feels her "biggest accomplishment, the one I am most proud of, is the way my children have turned out. I've always wanted to be a good mother." Having spent more than thirty years at Thomas Road Baptist Church, Jerry wishes to be remembered "as a successful pastor. . . . More important than that, I want to be remembered as a successful husband and father."

> *Macel and I will feel very fulfilled, if after fifty or sixty years of pulpit ministry, we have had the privilege of training scores of thousands of young men and young ladies to serve Christ and to change the world.*
>
> JERRY FALWELL

Despite the criticism and the tough times, Macel says that there is nothing she would do differently. During those trying times she would hold dear to the one passage of

Scripture that has guided her life, Psalm 121:1–2: "I will lift up mine eyes unto the hills, from whence cometh my help. My help cometh from the Lord." That is the one passage Macel says "I always keep on the tip of my tongue." Those words have been an ever present source of strength for Macel, especially during the dark days of her parents' deaths.

Parents, children, and, most important, husband—the words all speak of the family. For the last twenty-nine years Macel has had little ambition to be anything more than Mrs. Jerry Falwell, a preacher's wife. For her that is enough. Her close friend Shirley Burton put it best: "Macel once told me that she depended on no one for anything, except Jerry, and she depended on him for everything."

RUTH BELL GRAHAM

❧❧❧

Ours is by no way the usual marriage, but basic biblical
principles work in any marriage. . . . People ask me if I
did not suffer terribly from loneliness when Bill was away.
Occasionally I went to be with his tweed jacket for com-
pany.

RUTH GRAHAM

There certainly has been nothing usual about the marriage
of Ruth Bell Graham and Reverend Dr. William Franklin
Graham. But then there is nothing—absolutely nothing—
usual or common about these two people. Billy Graham, as
most of the world knows him, has been a confidant of
almost every U.S. President since Harry Truman. Along
with the Pope in Rome, he is without a doubt the best
known and most respected representative of the Christian
faith in the world.

As anyone knows who has heard him, Billy Graham has a
gift. It is the gift of preaching, of proclaiming the Gospel.
One Graham insider said, "When he gets up there in that
pulpit, something comes over him and he's very dynamic.
Even if you don't agree with what he says, you can't get
away from that power. Some well-known orators in the
future will study his tapes, even if they're not remotely
religious. They will review them to try to figure out what it
is that gives Billy that sort of power."

To date, evangelist Billy Graham has addressed more than ninety million people face to face and nearly two million people have come forward as inquirers at his Crusade meetings. In one service alone, in Seoul, Korea, he spoke to an audience of more than one million.

If anyone knows the secret to Dr. Graham's gift it is his wife, Ruth. Yet, in characteristic fashion, she is keeping that information well concealed; Ruth Graham is a woman who jealously guards her privacy.

Still, it was that gift that brought Bill and Ruth together for the first time. She first saw him as she sat on the steps of East Blanchard hall on the campus of Wheaton College in Illinois. "He's surely in a hurry," Ruth thought to herself. A few days later in Wheaton's Winston Hall the two saw each other again. The following Sunday morning, a group of students gathered for prayer before going out on Gospel team assignments. That morning Ruth heard a new voice pray. "There is a man who knows to Whom he is speaking," thought Ruth. That voice was strong and clear, with a passion and a mission.

Perhaps more than anything else, it is the merging of those two forces—passion and mission—that has characterized the lives of Ruth and Billy Graham. For Ruth, it has been a vibrant passion for life combined with a self-proclaimed streak of independence, and for Billy a passion to proclaim the Gospel and to always be on the go. Ruth once said that Bill "has to be on the move always, just to go somewhere, anywhere, but to go, to always be going and coming."

Billy Graham has been "going and coming" for almost four decades now. As he has circled the globe with the Gospel, he and Ruth have firmly established themselves in the hearts and minds of the American public as the "First Couple" of American Christianity. They have carved a place in the twentieth century that, most certainly, will remain unequaled.

LIKE FATHER, LIKE HUSBAND

Both Tammy Bakker and Macel Falwell have tried to steer clear of the typical role of minister's wife. Yet of all the seven women in this book, none is more unique than Ruth Graham. The word "unique" does not mean special or captivating, as it is commonly used, although both words can be used to describe Ruth. Unique means one and only one, and that is the best description of Ruth Graham.

As the daughter of medical missionaries to China, Ruth was steeped in the Christian faith. During those early days in China, Ruth saw firsthand two people who, despite adversity, refused to give in. Even with Japanese bombs dropping around them and gunfire in the distance, the family of Dr. Bell, Ruth's father, never became discouraged.

According to Patricia Cornwell, author of Mrs. Graham's best-selling biography, "Ruth tremendously admired her father, Dr. Bell. He was a well-known and well-respected doctor in China. Ruth just adored him. After having a father like that, I think she was looking for someone in a husband whom she could feel and admire in the same way. I'm not sure that there are a lot of men in the world that would hold her interest very long. She was used to a very strong man that she could look up to and admire. Billy fit those criteria."

Shortly after Ruth first heard the passion of a Billy Graham prayer, the couple were introduced. Within a month the couple had their first date—a Sunday afternoon presentation of the *Messiah*. Somehow as she sat next to Bill, listening to the music, she knew he was the one. Whether it was feminine instinct or spiritual insight, Ruth knew. In characteristic fashion, she "laid it before the Lord and left it there." The year was 1940, three years after Billy had preached his first sermon in a little plank-floored Baptist church in Florida.

I don't think we can ever see into the future. I did know when I first met Bill that God had His hand on him in a very special way. I don't really call it a premonition—I couldn't possibly have visualized what lay ahead. I'm glad I couldn't—I wouldn't have had the courage to marry him!

RUTH GRAHAM

The Bell-Graham romance continued for three years. It was anything but steady and there were times of sincere doubt. Finally, after their graduation from Wheaton College in 1943, Ruth Bell and Billy Graham were married. The ceremony took place on an August evening—Friday the thirteenth—in a stone chapel in the tiny mountain community of Montreat, North Carolina, carefully secluded in the Blue Ridge Mountains not far from where the Grahams now live.

That Sparkle in Her Eye

Throughout her life, Ruth Graham has had a seemingly limitless zest for life. "She has an almost girl-like spontaneity about her," says Patricia. "One of the most striking things about her is her eyes. They're so filled with light and they sparkle so much. And she has a rather oblique way of looking at things. She does what she feels like doing and if it seems rather eccentric to anybody else, that doesn't bother her in the least."

A favorite anecdote about Ruth Graham revolves around a microphone and, of all things, a mouse. Ruth was sitting in her living room, hooked up to an interviewer's tape recorder. "We'd been talking for almost eight solid hours and suddenly she fell silent and sort of squinted at something across the room. She took the microphone off her jacket, got up and went to the fireplace where she had a four-foot wrought-iron marshmallow fork—it looked like something out of the Tower of London, a horrible, macabre-looking thing.

"The next thing I know, she's on her hands and knees going across the floor with this fork and she starts jabbing it under the grandfather clock. Soon afterward, she produces this poor little gray mouse on the end of it. She's not saying a word, she's matter-of-fact about the way she's doing this. She opens the back door, sticks the fork out and you could hear the German shepherd chomping away at the mouse. She puts the fork back by the fireplace, sits back down on the couch, reattaches the microphone, and says, 'Now, where were we?' "

When asked, "From where did you gain your strong personality?" Ruth replied, "It's something of which I am not aware. I do not think of myself as strong—ornery and stubborn maybe, but not necessarily strong."

HANG GLIDING AND MOTORCYCLES

True to her nonconformist style, in mid-life Ruth Graham took up hang gliding and motorcycle riding. "I do love to go fast, to go full speed with the wind in my face," says Ruth. Those were the days when Billy's aides worked especially hard to keep a careful eye on her.

On one occasion Ruth's active lifestyle worked against her. She fell out of a tree. Her plan was to complete a pipe slide for her grandchildren then living in Mequon, Wisconsin. After a serious fall, Ruth landed in a hospital with one broken rib, a crushed vertebra, and a concussion. She was unconscious for a week. When she awoke, her memory was wiped clean of, among other things, one of her most prized possessions, the Bible verses she had memorized since childhood. Her recovery was painfully slow. As she was convalescing, Ruth wrote one of her daughters: "I have had difficulty reading anything—my Bible included—as my mind just wanders or won't absorb. I prayed, 'Lord, take anything from me, but please give me back my Bible verses.' "

In time Ruth did fully recover. According to doctors at Mayo Clinic, the fall had caused impairment of Ruth's short-term memory. It was probable that the fall and its related complications were also linked to problems Ruth later had with the left side of her body. Eventually, these difficulties culminated in the replacement of one hip and a portion of the joint in her wrist.

CURIOSITY AND COMPASSION

More than tree climbing and motorcycle riding, the essence of Ruth Graham can be found in two words—curiosity and compassion. Billy Graham's official biographer, John Pollock, writes, "more than anyone Ruth broadened Graham's mind. She had no need to polish his manners . . . but she was cultured and traveled, and had an enormous love of art and literature."

Ruth's curiosity was fostered with her childhood study of the Bible. "I had, as it were, cut my teeth on the Bible, and do not recall a time when I did not love it." When interviewed by Julie Nixon Eisenhower, Ruth commented, "It's surprising that there aren't more inconsistencies in the Bible. So many different people wrote it. And from so many different points of view. It's the differences that make it valid."

In keeping with her appreciation of diversity, Ruth maintains her membership with the Presbyterian church. It hasn't been easy. Year after year, there have been endless attempts by well-meaning "friends" to convert her to her husband's Southern Baptist denomination.

"When two people agree on everything, one of them is unnecessary." In marriage "if you agree on everything, there's not going to be much growth for either one."

RUTH GRAHAM

Along with curiosity, perhaps it is compassion which most characterizes Ruth Graham. One close friend suggests that to understand Ruth you have to grasp "her great compassion for other people. She has chosen to serve others behind the scenes—to live her own life trying to help people." She's been known to have people in her home that many wouldn't allow in their yards. These include children from the nearby juvenile detention center and drug addicts with habits to kick.

Then there was the young prostitute Ruth befriended, as well as convicts on death row. One death row inmate was once in Ruth's Sunday school class. In time he left Ruth's class and committed murder in Detroit. Ruth visited him in prison, sent him classical music tapes, and consistently wrote him. Yet still she told him, "What you did is wrong and you have to be punished for it, but that doesn't mean that you're a worthless person." Most often, these expressions of concern were carried on beyond the public's eye; Ruth didn't want them to appear as publicity stunts.

Los Angeles, London, and New York

As much as any wife of the evangelists, Ruth Graham has been her husband's closest adviser. Yet unlike Maude Aimee Humbard or Frances Swaggart, Ruth Graham chose not to take an active role in the running of her husband's evangelistic association. Rather, "what she's done for the most part is what she's done for him," comments Patricia. "She's largely responsible for making him the person he is. She's given him good guidance over the years."

I almost stand in awe of him and yet I'm not afraid of him. To be with Bill in this type of work won't be easy. But somehow I need Bill.

                                        RUTH GRAHAM

An early example of Ruth's keen guidance took place at Billy's famous 1949 Los Angeles Crusade. That Crusade, originally scheduled for three weeks, extended to eight weeks with attendance topping 350,000 people. Billy Graham's first message was based on Jonathan Edwards's sermon "Sinners in the Hands of an Angry God." Billy chose to read large parts of the message; few listeners felt it "went over too well." Afterward Ruth said, "You've got to stick with the Bible. That is your source of power."

As the Crusade went on and on, Billy had almost run out of sermons. When Ruth came to visit him he was begging sermon outlines from preacher friends, and reading every recommended book he could get his hands on. "I remember his desperate straits in Los Angeles," says Ruth. "Probably the best thing that ever happened to him—this suddenly having to get down and study, especially the Bible. He was thrown back on simple, straight biblical preaching."

Through the years, "Ruth has always kept Billy on track about that," says Patricia Cornwell. "When he gets up there and says, 'The Bible says . . .'—that's the source of his power."

Not knowing she is talking to Ruth Graham, a woman asks her, "I wonder what it would be like waking up in the morning married to that man." That man was Billy Graham. Ruth quickly replied, "It's something I've been doing for a number of years now, and it's quite pleasant."

In the 1954 Greater London Crusade and the 1957 New York Crusade, Ruth was again at Billy's side for guidance. Both Crusades were breakthroughs for the Graham team— London as their first international meeting and New York as the first coast-to-coast telecast of a Crusade service.

During these great Crusades, Ruth's help was more for emotional support than problem-solving. In Britain especially, Billy needed Ruth; his welcome there was far from enthusiastic. One weekend gazette with a huge circulation lambasted the Reverend Graham as "Silly Billy." Others made light of Billy's preaching style and his American roots. As Billy and Ruth were preparing to leave for the nearby meeting place, an aide called to inform the Graham team that the arena was barely a fifth full. And that was the good news—even worse were the scores of newspaper photographers snapping photos of the empty seats.

"If a devoted mate was ever necessary this was the time," recalls Billy. "I was a sorry case of nerves. I kept thinking how miserably I had failed. Ruth gave me the sense of confidence I so badly needed. She reminded me that people all over the world were praying for us." As Ruth and Billy entered Harringay Arena, the lobby was deserted. Inside the arena it was a different story. Every seat was taken and thousands were standing in the street on the other side of the building, eagerly waiting for Billy's sermons.

In 1957 the Protestant Council of the City of New York invited Billy to conduct a revival in that great city. Although he had long desired to take the Gospel to New York, he told Ruth, "I go in fear and trembling. I'm going to be crucified by my critics, but I feel I must go." As Ruth had done so many times before, she gave him the strength he needed.

During that ninety-seven-day Crusade, the Grahams enjoyed almost unprecedented coverage in the New York papers. With typically comprehensive style, the New York *Times* chose to publish the entire forty-five-minute text of Billy Graham's first sermon. One columnist, writing a five-part biography of Graham, described Billy and his wife as a "dazzling advertisement for the state of matrimony." And the *Herald Tribune*, which had recently begun to run pictures of attractive girls on their front page, decided it was the perfect time to use a photograph of Mrs. Graham. In response, one reader wrote, "At long last I have a pinup that I think the Lord approves."

TRAIN STATIONS AND AIRPORTS

During Billy's endless travels, Ruth has been his constant source of support and most trusted companion. "Neither Ruth nor I enjoyed being separated any more than other couples who are in love. Being away from her was the most difficult thing I've had to do. After she'd leave me at the train station or airport, I'd feel like crying. I just couldn't bear to think of being three or four weeks without her."

One story illustrates the price the Grahams paid for Billy's tireless spreading of the Gospel. During the 1949 Los Angeles Crusade, Ruth left her children in the caring hands of her family. There were only two children then—Gigi and Anne. Toward the end of the long Crusade there was a knock on their door. When Ruth opened it, her sister and brother-in-law were standing outside holding her daughter Anne. Anne, however, didn't know her mother. Ruth stretched out her arms to her daughter, but small Anne hid her face against her aunt's neck.

That night Anne sobbed for her aunt; she had forgotten that Ruth was her mother. It was worse when she saw her father; she didn't know Billy either.

Ruth tried to stay at home with her growing family as much as possible. Yet even though distance separated Billy from Ruth, in many ways he was still emotionally dependent on her. One twenty-year friend recalls, "It would be typical every single night, even if Billy were on the other side of the world, that the phone would ring. It would be Bill and she would be quiet, listening to him tell her what he had been doing. Then she would say something encouraging or something about the children. She was always a source of warmth and encouragement.

"It would have been easy for someone in her position to say, 'Look, now it's my turn. The roof is leaking and the furnace isn't working and I haven't seen you in five months and I'm not in a very good mood.' But she's not like that,

PORTRAIT GALLERY

Tammy Faye Bakker

Macel Falwell

Ruth Bell Graham

Maude Aimee Humbard

Oral and Evelyn Roberts

Arvella and Robert Schuller

Frances Swaggart

she's never done that." Rather, Ruth Graham is a listener and a thinker; she's not a talker. "More than reading . . . more than voices in conversation, I just love to hear the wind in the trees," says Ruth. "I love to hear the birds. And mostly, I just love to listen to silence."

The disparity between listening and talking is one of the differences between Ruth and Billy. According to a long-time neighbor, "Ruth always mentions this, he's a talker. He will talk and he's accustomed to people listening to him. She's the opposite, she's more of a listener. If you really have something to say, she will listen for two straight hours and not say a word. She thinks it's better for her to listen than to give an opinion."

> *Bill is primarily a man's man. All his close personal friends are men. I would like to see Bill more often, to cook his favorite dishes, and help him buy his clothes—but all that is done by his staff.*
>
> RUTH GRAHAM

Billy Graham also has a stronger, more outgoing, driven personality than Ruth. Because of Billy's extensive travels "he can talk intelligently on almost any topic." Ruth, on the other hand, "always has something to say, yet most often she has a very quiet presence." Ruth particularly dislikes interviews and has been known to have a mental Rolodex of prepared responses for reporters' questions. She once was asked, "Why do you hate being interviewed?" Her response: "The truth is, I'm not so sure I hate it; I think I like talking too much and I'm afraid of what I might say."

There definitely have been times when Ruth Graham has been very outspoken and opinionated. She would be mortified, however, if she ever did anything to hurt her husband. On one occasion, she sent caution to the wind. On May 20, 1975, Ruth was arrested.

It happened during a speech delivered by President Gerald Ford in Charlotte, North Carolina's Freedom Park.

Around the small lake and the band shell there was a crowd of seventy-five thousand people, including scores of protesters. Ruth was sitting in the front row, next to the center aisle in an area roped off for security purposes. Midway through Ford's speech a barefoot young man, carrying a concealed sign, made his way to the front. Unfortunately for him, his destination landed him next to Ruth.

As he lifted the protest sign above his head, Ruth rose from her seat and snatched it from his hands. It was a spontaneous, practical decision. She sat down and placed the sign on the ground with her white pumps firmly planted on it. The man was startled and asked for the sign to be returned. Ruth merely shook her head and smiled. Soon police officers arrived to escort the protester away.

When the young protester learned the identity of his "assailant" he filed a warrant for Ruth's arrest, charging assault and battery. On August 29 the case went to trial. For the most part it was a charade. After forty-five minutes the case was dismissed for lack of evidence. That night Richard Nixon called Ruth to congratulate her, as did President Gerald Ford two nights later. Jokingly Ruth asked President Ford, "Don't you want to hire me full time as a sign-snatcher?" "I'll place you in the front row," he replied.

Too Friendly Visitors

With Billy's busy schedule, Ruth knew that separations from him would be frequent. If she was to be without her husband, she reasoned she should at least be allowed to live where she was happiest. For forty years that location has been the small mountain community of Montreat, North Carolina.

Montreat is a quiet retreat center for the Presbyterian Church. There is only one road in and out of town. And you don't go through Montreat. You drive in a two-lane road, circle the small pond, and drive out the same road. This small North Carolina community is far—very far—from the fast lane, and that's the way Ruth Graham likes it.

The Grahams lived on that main road in and out of Montreat for several years. As Billy's popularity grew, so did the courage of curious sightseers. Often they peered in the kitchen window to see what Ruth was cooking, stopped to pick flowers for souvenirs, or snapped photographs of the children. Those were the days when the adventurous Graham children would ask payment for photographs or draw a rope across the road and charge passing cars a toll. Those who stopped expected to see the children with halos encircling their heads. But Ruth has always been more of a realist. She once referred to her family as "Noah's Ark of happy confusion."

Although the family learned to cope, Ruth recalls that the visitors were often terribly annoying. Eventually it became a family joke. "I'd claim that if the sightseeing cars drove quickly by, they were probably from the Episcopal center. If they slowed down, they were Presbyterians. Then there were the ones that actually stopped, got out of their cars and wandered all over. They were the Baptists. Bill used to kid me that I was prejudiced against the Baptists. But that's the way they were. They were so friendly. Sometimes, too friendly!"

DIRT SLIDES AND MOTHERHOOD

Eventually, the decision was made to move. While Ruth stayed out of Billy's evangelistic operations, when it came to building a new home she ran the entire show. The Grahams had located a picturesque 200-acre plot at the edge of the Blue Ridge Mountains. When Billy was on the West Coast, Ruth's frustrations with visitors drove her to head to the bank, borrow the money, and buy the land. Billy knew little of the transaction until his return.

It was time to move to the mountain.

Besides her faith and her love for her family, Ruth's

greatest passion is for her house and that mountain she lives on. With Billy gone so much of the time, she carved out her own life on that mountain, reading, taking long walks, and raising her family.

Patricia explains: "There's hardly anything she'd rather do than be in that house sitting before a fire reading something, writing poetry or talking with somebody. That is her refuge and it's a manifestation of herself. She put herself into the building of that home. She scrounged for the antiques and the old wood, and she forged it in a way with her own imagination."

It was on that mountain that Ruth raised her five children —Franklin, Ed, Gigi, Anne, and Ruth. On the long Sunday afternoons, she would bring the children together to listen to their father on the "Hour of Decision" broadcast, and then in the evening give them Bible games or Bible coloring books. There was most always an open Bible within reach—on the stove, atop a porch table, or in her hand as she completed the housework.

As with all the seven women in this book, the times with the children were the most special for Ruth, especially when they were small. It's those everyday times of closeness and sharing that she holds most dear. The best times were "when one would climb on my bed and talk things over, or spending weekends on our mountain property, or welcoming a new little Graham into the family."

> *I treasure those years. They were the times of unbelievable bliss when a little, snugly wrapped bundle would be laid in my arms. . . .*
>
> RUTH GRAHAM

A simple story illustrates Ruth's love for her family and her mountain. "Once we made a steep dirt slide way up above the house in the woods. It was fall and the earth was dry and crispy with fallen leaves. We would start at the top and slide on our seats all the way down. Then we'd scramble back up and repeat the fun, laughing and shouting all the way, arriving back at the house filthy, exhausted, and happy."

When Ruth does grant an occasional interview, she emphasizes the critical importance of a mother's role. She told one interviewer, "I have told my children I don't want anyone putting on my tombstone, 'She might as well have traveled.' " She adds, "I am a strong believer in women's lib, to this extent: I think women should be liberated from civic responsibility, from having to work for a living, and unless it's absolutely necessary, from all extracurricular affairs. They need to be liberated from them so they can devote themselves to their homes."

Next to her family and her mountain home, Ruth Graham's passion is for missions. She grew up surrounded by the love and courage of missionaries. She was convinced that the highest and noblest expression of love for God was to follow in their footsteps. At the age of twelve, Ruth dreamed of becoming a spinster missionary to the nomads of Tibet.

Life, of course, took a different turn for this spinster missionary. In an interview in *Ladies' Home Journal* Ruth commented, "All my life, I had felt called for mission work there in China, and I only came to college to prepare myself for that work. But I think the Lord must have given me that intense longing for a purpose, so that I could have the understanding and the sense of fulfillment that I now receive from Bill's work. I knew from the beginning that I wouldn't be in first place in his life. Christ would be first. Knowing that, accepting that, solves an awful lot of problems right there. So I can watch him go with no regrets, and wait for him joyfully."

TOGETHER THROUGH LAUGHTER AND SORROW

While Ruth waited for Billy, all was not joy and laughter. As with Macel Falwell, one of the most difficult times for

Ruth was the loss of her parents. Their deaths left a great void in her life. Reminders of her parents filled Ruth's mountain home: her mother's old wheelchair, her father's battered hat on the bookshelf, and then there were the many personal items from years of missionary work in China. The worst times were the cold early mornings when she awoke alone. Bill was gone, but with comfort she quickly thought, "But Mother and Daddy are home." Then she remembered; she indeed was alone.

Even through difficult times like these, Ruth has kept her keen sense of humor. It's proved to be a good way to cope with life's unexpected troubles. Early in their courtship, Billy told Ruth he wanted to meet Dr. and Mrs. Bell. Ruth arranged for the meeting and warned Bill that the area they lived in was filled with hillbillies. As part of the ploy, Ruth pulled down her long, dark hair, blackened a tooth, took off her shoes, and headed down the road barefoot to meet him. Unfortunately, Ruth had disguised herself so well, Bill drove straight by her.

Ruth also enjoys poking fun at people who take themselves too seriously. One nonstop-talking dinner guest received an unexpected appetizer. He anticipated soup, but when he looked down he discovered he had been served a bowl of muddy water with tadpoles swimming in it. He was about to continue with his favorite subject—himself—when he looked down and discovered the contents of his bowl. Quickly he set down his spoon and remained quiet the remainder of the evening.

One of the most difficult times for Billy was "Watergate" in the early 1970s. "The whole situation," says Ruth, "was the hardest thing that Bill has ever gone through personally." Richard Nixon and Billy Graham had been close friends since the mid-fifties. The friendship had grown very close during the Eisenhower administration, when Nixon was Vice President. As the Watergate scandal emerged, Graham was deeply dismayed. Yet, during the early months he continued to stand up for his longtime friend Richard

Nixon. In part, Billy thought, the ordeal was caused by overkill from the media.

In May 1974 the Watergate tapes came out. Billy was shocked. For the first time he learned of a man who was a stranger to the evangelist. It was almost as if there were two personalities in Richard Nixon: the man Billy had known and the totally different person on the tapes. Eventually, Graham issued a statement repudiating Nixon's behavior, but refusing to forsake his longtime friend.

A PASSION TO PREACH

The struggles of Watergate have long passed for the Grahams, and Billy has been careful not to mix his mission with politics. For his entire life, Billy Graham's mission and his passion have been to spread the Gospel. It is that passion to preach and his strength of leadership which Ruth has most admired.

During the early months of Ruth and Billy's courtship the two often talked back and forth of their future plans. Finally Billy stopped the conversation and asked, "Do you or do you not think the Lord brought us together?" "Yes," she replied. "Then, I'll do the leading and you'll do the following."

Billy has been leading ever since. He has been leading Ruth, his family, and almost the entire Christian faith as its most respected Protestant spokesman. During the four decades Billy Graham has taken the Christian faith to the world, he has achieved unequaled accomplishments. In 1950, he launched the Billy Graham Evangelistic Association with a shoebox filled with $25,000. That same year he launched the "Hour of Decision" radio program. With fifteen million listeners, it enjoyed the largest audience of any religious program in history. In 1960, the Graham team founded *Decision* magazine and four years later helped launch *Christianity Today.*

Since the famous 1957 New York City service, Billy has

been best known for his televised Crusades. "Bill's job is to reach the greatest number of people possible in the most direct way," says Ruth. "And the most direct way is a Crusade. You can reach people that way who would never set foot in a Crusade."

No one else has mastered the power of the crusade and of television as well as Billy Graham. The evangelist adds, "It's almost as if I'm not even aware of the thousands and thousands of people out there. I'm preaching just to the first six inches in front of my face. I feel almost totally alone. And even if nobody responded, if no one came, I would still preach."

For Billy, the climax of his mission and the most passionate part of his preaching is the invitation. "At the invitation, in the five or the ten minutes that this appeal lasts, is when most of my strength leaves me," says the evangelist. "I don't know what it is, but something is going out of me at that moment."

More than anything else, it is the strength of those few minutes that Billy guards most carefully. As he ages, Billy has said that what he fears most is "for the passion to be gone—like it happened with others in their old age in the Bible. For the fire to go."

As long as Ruth is there by his side, with her curiosity, compassion and wit, there is little doubt that the passion will stay. "I'd rather have a little bit of Bill, than a lot of any other man," says Ruth. Scores of millions most certainly would agree. They can be thankful that the Reverend Dr. William Franklin Graham had the passion and stayed true to his mission. And like Ruth Bell Graham, "the spinster missionary to China," they can be thankful they had just "a little bit of Bill."

MAUDE AIMEE HUMBARD

⁂

I love television. I think it's a window to your soul.
There's something in your eyes that's either sincere or not.
Rex and I can go onto television, and they see two people
that really have love and a ray of hope. In many ways we
were the first.

MAUDE AIMEE HUMBARD

Here are four questions to ponder:

1. Who has had the number-one-rated television program in all America?
2. Who was first to bring a weekly church service to U.S. homes?
3. Who was first to regularly televise Protestant Sunday morning church services on an international scale?
4. Who, perhaps, has had the greatest impact on Christian mass-media evangelism by encouraging Oral Roberts and Jimmy Swaggart to go on television, and has helped expand Jerry Falwell's television ministry?

If you answered Rex Humbard to each question, you were half right. If you answered Rex and Maude Aimee Humbard, you were completely right. Consider these accomplishments:

On a weekly basis, Rex and Maude Aimee Humbard have ministered to some one hundred million people. The weekly television program which bears Rex's name has been telecast by more than six hundred stations, is regularly translated into six foreign languages and broadcast around the world through two thousand feeder satellite stations. Through efforts like these, the Humbards by 1970 had the number one evangelical show in America.

"I never gave up because Rex has a destiny," says Maude Aimee. "From the time of Rex's birth, God planned a special place for him in the Kingdom. Rex was to be the first man to fulfill the Great Commission literally: never before had one man gone into all the world preaching the gospel."

Rex was not the only person who had a destiny—so did Maude Aimee. "My mother told me from the time I was at the point of remembering that I was going to be a special child. She said, "You're going to do great things for God." And she has.

GROWING UP TEXAN STYLE

Named for the famous evangelist Aimee Semple McPherson, Maude Aimee Jones was born to a wealthy Dallas family. Her Texan home had twenty-five rooms and came with maids, servants, and gardeners. Unfortunately this early good life was short-lived. When Maude Aimee was only fifteen months old, her father abandoned the family, including her brother Charles who was then eleven.

Mr. Jones took all the family money with him. Overnight the rest of the family's lives changed. To make ends meet, the bedrooms in the large house were rented for five dollars. Mrs. Jones struggled for groceries. "We never went hungry and I never did without clothes," says Maude Aimee. "I don't know how she did it."

Long before Maude Aimee's arrival, the Joneses' house had become known as the "House of Preachers." "Any preacher that came to town knew there was room for him and plenty of food," recalls Maude Aimee. It was through this friendship with traveling evangelists that Maude Aimee and Charles soon had a substitute family. Albert Ott came to pastor at the Joneses' church, and he and his wife became "Pappa and Mommie" to Maude Aimee. "They gave us back the joy of being loved as a family," Maude Aimee recalls with fondness.

Reverend Ott started a Saturday radio broadcast as soon as he took over at Maude Aimee's church, Bethel Temple. Later he expanded to daily programs. Maude Aimee loved to sing, and by the age of eight she was singing at most Sunday church meetings and nightly revival services.

Because of her dedication to church, Maude Aimee's life became very different from her schoolmates. Besides her singing, when Pastor Ott conducted a building drive, it was young Maude Aimee who raised the most money. She did it by shining shoes in front of the corner drugstore. Even at that early age, Maude Aimee was fulfilling the family motto: "Don't do anything halfway for God."

KEEPING THE FAMILY MOTTO

Maude Aimee has lived that family motto every day of her life. Of all the evangelists' wives, no one is more committed and more driven than she. Whatever it takes, whoever it takes, however long it takes—Maude Aimee will get the job done. You can ask anyone in the Humbard ministry and they'll agree. She's a driven woman.

At the early age of fifteen, Maude Aimee already knew she had this talent. At a Valentine's Day party, she rigged a drawing so she and Rex could spend the evening together. "That was a little sneaky," admits Maude Aimee, but "I've never really been a conniver. I always manage to find my way of doing what I want done and getting it done just the way I want it. It must be a God-given trait, because I still do it to this day. I get there."

Rex is much more easygoing. It's easy to see the difference between Maude Aimee and her husband; it's in their eyes. Maude Aimee has an intensity that is unmistakable, while Rex is relaxed. In any picture, with your thumb and forefinger you can cover their faces, and the eyes tell it all. Only daughter Elizabeth explains it this way: "Dad is a dreamer, a visionary, but Mom made sure his dreams came true. She's a driver. She's breathed the fear of God in every employee. Yet she's very encouraging, and she's very honest."

> *I'm a straightforward person, and I say exactly what I think. It may hurt to hear it, but at least nobody wonders what I think.*
>
> MAUDE AIMEE HUMBARD

Elizabeth calls this quality "spunk"; Maude Aimee simply calls it "bullheadedness." "Sometimes I'm known as 'Old Battle-Ax' because I look after the details and see that things get done. If you're doing anything for the Lord, if you're not going to do it right, then don't make a mess. Just don't even attempt it. My mother and brother used to say, 'It's a good thing you married her, Rex, because only you and God could live with her.'"

LOVE AT FIRST SIGHT

Rex and Maude Aimee have been man and wife for almost forty-five years. Her marriage, says Maude Aimee, is the "simplest thing I've ever had to do. You don't work at something that you really love. I love my husband, and he loves me. I've never doubted his love for a minute."

That love first sparked at the Texas State Fairgrounds Auditorium in 1939. "I knew the minute I laid eyes on Rex that he was God's and he was mine." Yet like most everything in her life, nothing came easy.

That winter of 1939 the singing Humbard family was slated to sing at a March of Dimes benefit program for President Franklin D. Roosevelt's birthday celebration. The Humbard Singers included young Alpha Rex Emmanuel

Humbard. On the same program was fifteen-year-old Maude Aimee Jones.

Rex was about to join his family on stage when he found himself staring at "one of the most attractive girls I had ever seen." Quickly he took the hand of his three-year-old sister Juanita and led her to the attractive girl, Maude Aimee Jones. "If you're not going on stage right away," said Rex to Maude Aimee, "would you mind keeping an eye on my baby sister while we sing our number?" Maude Aimee said she'd be glad to, and Rex went to join his family on stage. Even at her young age, Maude Aimee knew that Rex Humbard was "something special."

By the next morning Reverend Ott and V. O. Stamps had agreed on a plan to keep the Humbards in Dallas for the next two years. Most weeks that meant twenty-eight radio broadcasts, in addition to two Sunday services and one Wednesday service at Bethel Temple. More importantly to Rex Humbard, it provided two years to get to know Miss Maude Aimee Jones, the girl he had fallen in love with that night at the State Fairgrounds Auditorium.

This classic "boy meets girl" story was not to have a happy ending for three years. Rex's father had accepted a church position in Little Rock, Arkansas, and Rex was needed to organize the church meetings and promote them on radio. Three hundred miles was an expansive separation in those days, and Maude Aimee was convinced that Rex was seeing someone else. She broke off the engagement, leaving both of them miserable.

In time the relationship mended itself. It culminated with a wedding performed before 8,500 people in the summer of 1942.

That summer the Humbards were invited to host a meeting at Cadle Tabernacle in Indianapolis, Indiana. Rex's mother extended an invitation to Maude Aimee to join them and she did, with her mother's blessings of course. The first night of those services Maude Aimee remembers seeing two hundred young women longingly looking up at

Rex. Girls were always attracted to Rex because he was a handsome, charming, and dynamic speaker. Maude Aimee feared things would never be the same between them.

Rex, however, had other plans. That night he asked Maude Aimee if they couldn't pick up where they had left off. She said yes. One week later they exchanged their wedding vows in front of those 8,500 faithful in Cadle Tabernacle. "We couldn't afford to go back to Texas and have the kind of wedding I dreamed of," said Maude Aimee. So, after Sunday night services on August 2, 1942, Rex invited the congregation to a wedding. Maude Aimee remembers hearing two hundred young women sigh as Rex said, "I do."

> *I told my husband I'd live with him in a tent when he asked me to marry him. He was so poor we couldn't afford a house. But I said I'd rather live with a man I loved than to live in luxury.*
>
> MAUDE AIMEE HUMBARD

A POSTAGE STAMP HOME

Two days after they were married, the Rex Humbards rented their first home. It consisted of three rooms on the second floor of an old house in South Bend, Indiana. For Maude Aimee, marriage was an eye-opener. "I had never done a load of laundry in my life. I did not know how to cook. I didn't even know how to boil water." For survival purposes, Rex taught his new wife to cook.

At the time the entire Humbard family was enjoying a successful stay in South Bend, where the crowds were so big that the police had to block off the streets. It was in nearby Mishiwaka, Indiana, that the newest Humbards celebrated their one-month wedding "anniversary." Forty years later, they still celebrate their wedding on the second of every month.

Rex and Maude Aimee soon headed south to the Carolinas. It was in Greenville, South Carolina, that Rex was ordained by the International Ministerial Foundation. Maude Aimee found out she was pregnant shortly thereafter.

From Greenville, the Humbards traveled on to Gastonia, North Carolina, and Louisville, Kentucky. Maude Aimee dearly wanted to be near her mother in Dallas for the birth of their first child. That first child, Alpha Rex Emmanuel Humbard, Jr., arrived on October 19, 1943. Two days after the birth, Rex was back on the road again, leaving Maude Aimee and Rex Jr. in the capable hands of Maude Aimee's mother.

It became apparent to the Humbards by then that they could no longer just pick up and rent a room wherever they were preaching, especially now that they had a young baby. Maude Aimee had her heart set on a sixteen-foot trailer, with a living room, bedroom, and kitchen "about the size of a postage stamp." That trailer, and others slightly larger, would be the Humbard family home for the next ten years.

After the birth of Rex Jr., Maude Aimee and her husband seriously considered adopting. Maude Aimee's first childbirth experience was difficult, and her mother warned against a repeat performance. The Humbards began their efforts to adopt a baby girl. However, as their plans unfolded, Maude Aimee discovered she was again pregnant. "I eagerly awaited my own baby daughter," remembers Maude Aimee. "Everything I bought was for a girl." The little girl the Humbards expected turned out to be a beautiful boy whom they named Don Raymond. They affectionately called him "Sunshine" because he was always smiling. He joined the family in a new trailer home, a twenty-five-footer this time. That trailer was now home to Rex, Maude Aimee, Rex Jr., Don and Maude Aimee's mother, who lived with the young Humbards off and on for twelve years.

My children, Lord knows, they've been dragged from one side of the United States to the other, sleeping in the back of cars. We had meetings every night for twelve years. My children never knew what a home or house was.

MAUDE AIMEE HUMBARD

JOYS AND JEALOUSIES

It wasn't until twelve years later that Maude Aimee finally delivered the newborn girl she had earlier anticipated. It was 1959, and the Cathedral of Tomorrow had been open for a year. Rex Jr. was sixteen and Don was twelve by then, "both good boys," according to their mother. The church was busy, and Rex still traveled, but not as much as he had in the early years.

"I was thirty-eight years old, the same age when I gave birth that my mother was when I was born. It was somewhat unusual to have a child that late in life, but the fever caught on at the Cathedral. During the months that I carried Elizabeth, forty-one children were born in that church." It became a joke that it was dangerous to drink from the Cathedral water fountain. " 'Disconnect that thing,' we used to say, 'or we'll overrun the nurseries.' "

No child was more eagerly anticipated than Aimee Elizabeth, who was born on October 1, 1959. Her birth made front-page headlines and triggered 3,800 congratulation cards. "Elizabeth dearly filled a place of love in our home," says Maude Aimee. She was determined to "enjoy this child," even though she was still very active in the ministry and traveled to Cleveland every morning to tape the Humbard television program.

Elizabeth seemed destined for a role in the ministry from the beginning. When she was only eighteen months old, she was already announcing on Rex's nightly broadcast. At four she started school and began appearing on stage. She didn't start singing until she was twelve years old. Elizabeth remembers: "Connie Smith, the singer, was appearing at a New Year's Eve telethon sponsored by our church. When she sang, it was like magic." Elizabeth bought all of Connie's records and practiced singing with them. Six weeks later, she told her parents, "I'm going to sing."

And sing she did, almost every Sunday since then. At thirteen she began touring with the family. "I enjoyed the touring," says Elizabeth. "What was hard was coming home." However, there came a time when the joy left. Elizabeth became jealous of the ministry because it took her parents away from her. "Holidays were hard and birthdays."

In her early high school years, she rebelled against being a "preacher's kid." "We were doing big work in a small town, and I felt everyone was watching me." Elizabeth's rebellion was aimed more at Maude Aimee than her father. Elizabeth's parents finally pulled her out of school to travel along with the family, and hopefully away from her problems.

> *There was a period of about two years when it was hard to say, "I love you" to Mom and Dad, Elizabeth says with feeling. I felt as if my friends had been taken away from me.*
>
> AIMEE ELIZABETH HUMBARD

When Elizabeth was fifteen, she found her own peace. It came on the night she made her own commitment of faith. No longer was it her parents' faith; it was now hers. "Richard Hogue was preaching, and something he said really touched me. I found myself walking towards the altar—I just had to get there. Suddenly all the negative feelings I had, all the bitterness came rushing out. Elizabeth was totally unashamed of her commitment but was nervous about telling her parents, who were out of town at the time. When she did, though, Maude Aimee and Rex were thrilled. "I felt a special closeness to my parents after that," Elizabeth recalls. "And I still feel it."

Elizabeth was not slated to be the youngest Humbard. At the age of forty-two, Maude Aimee became pregnant again.

The son, as it turned out to be, was to be named Charley, in honor of her brother and father.

While Maude Aimee was in the hospital awaiting the birth of her third son, another scene was being played across town with her second son. Don, then a high school senior, was playing in a varsity football game when suddenly his neck was broken. Maude Aimee immediately stopped her labor pains. "I will never have another pain until I see my son walk out of this hospital," she told the nurses.

A neurosurgeon attending the game that night is credited with saving Don's life. Ten days after the accident, Don walked out of the hospital. Within the hour Maude Aimee's labor pains began anew. Charley was born a few hours later.

Elizabeth and Charley were raised much differently than their two older brothers. Rex Jr. and Don were raised on the road. Their siblings had a more typical upbringing, even though Rex and Maude Aimee continued their travels. Don was at home while both Elizabeth and Charley were young, and he became a sort of "fill-in" father to both of them. "I can remember Don feeding us and taking care of us when we were sick," recalls Elizabeth. "He provided the family atmosphere we needed back then."

RADIO PIONEERS

Years before the family had included four children, Rex and Maude Aimee began their climb into broadcasting fame. It started in Nashville, Tennessee. There Rex met up with an old friend, Jack Wolier, then the program director at WSIX, a local radio station.

Jack originally had given the Humbards their start in radio back in Hot Springs, Arkansas. To promote the Humbards' gospel meeting in town, he now arranged for them to perform on two daily radio programs on WSIX. However, after three weeks the broadcast was canceled.

The WSIX management thought the Humbards weren't attracting enough listeners.

Rex and Jack set out to prove the station management wrong. They printed a postcard with a picture of the Humbard Gospel Group on it, and offered it free to all those who requested it. Within twelve hours, the station had received 4,982 mailed requests, and by the end of the next day, that number had soared to 8,200.

Thanks to that response, the Humbards not only stayed on the air in Nashville, but the Mutual Network offered the family five radio programs a week. Later the network canceled two of those programs, prompting Rex to visit New York in hopes of restoring the five-day-a-week schedule. Although the Humbards weren't paid anything for their shows, the exposure, they felt, brought people to their meetings.

Rex succeeded in New York. He convinced NBC's Blue Network to broadcast the Humbard program coast to coast and to pay them four hundred dollars a week for the privilege. The Humbards now had a year's contract and were able to broadcast their shows from the cities where they were holding their revivals.

At the end of that contract year, the Humbards' contract with NBC came up for renewal. NBC was happy to sign them for another year, but with one slight change. The network had been paying the bills for the last twelve months, and now they had a commercial sponsor for the show—Carter's Little Liver Pills. The Humbards said thanks, but no thanks—theirs was a religious program, and they felt they couldn't serve the Lord and advertise liver pills too. For the time being, it seemed that the Humbard broadcasting career had come to an end.

Almost Queen for a Day

Like their good friends Jim and Tammy Bakker, Rex and Maude Aimee have a lifetime of stories recounting their ministering years on the road. One such story came about new Los Angeles, California. The Humbards were in Los Angeles to conduct services at the Angeles Temple, the five thousand-seat auditorium built by evangelist Aimee Semple McPherson. "We were holding services there on the first anniversary of her death. Angeles Temple had not been filled since she died until we came. And we packed it," Maude Aimee says.

While in California the Humbards stayed in a trailer park in nearby Pomona. "At that time, there was a television program in Hollywood called 'Queen for a Day,'" says Maude Aimee, "and I told these ladies in the trailer park how I would love to go on that show."

> *The question on the program was this: "If you were queen for a day, what would you like to do?" And I said, "I haven't had a bath in twelve years, and I would like to have a bath."*
>
> MAUDE AIMEE HUMBARD

Trailer homes in the 1950s didn't have all the conveniences of modern mobile homes. In fact, for ten years the Humbards didn't have a shower let alone a bath in any of the trailers they owned. Usually they parked in a facility that included showers. "A bath would have been a luxury to me," recalls Maude Aimee.

"We all went down to see 'Queen for a Day' one day, all us ladies from the trailer park, and one of the ladies stole my line. Of course, they chose her to appear on the show. I never did get my bath."

It was the year after that, that the Humbards confronted their first family crisis. Rex Jr. had been examined and found to have advanced tuberculosis. Two thirds of his lung had collapsed. The Humbards were advised by doctors to place him in a sanitarium as soon as possible. Instead, Maude Aimee followed the advice of her brother Charles and took Rex Jr. to be prayed for by a Tulsa evangelist. The Humbards had never heard of this new evangelist. His name was Oral Roberts.

Oral was about to open a tent meeting in Mobile, Alabama, and Charles offered to notify the evangelist of the Humbards' arrival. When the Humbards walked into the services, Oral placed his hands on Rex Jr. and asked God to heal the boy. After this simple act, Oral advised Rex and Maude Aimee, "Go now and don't worry. The Lord has done the job."

Maude Aimee remembers that Rex Jr. stopped coughing almost immediately. For four weeks he seemed to grow stronger and more active. The Humbards then followed Oral to Tampa, Florida, where Maude Aimee took Rex Jr. to a new doctor to be examined. "The doctor examined him, took X rays, and then asked me, 'Why are you here? There's nothing wrong with your son.' I answered, 'This is the reason,' and I showed him the X rays from before. Finally he responded, 'Something's happened to your son.'"

Something had indeed happened to Rex Jr. "Yes, we had him prayed for," said Maude Aimee. The amazing thing was that there were no scar tissues, no lingering evidence of the disease, and, best of all, Rex Jr. had been cured.

That early experience began a lifelong friendship between the Humbards and the Robertses. "We have a nice relationship . . . as close as I guess you could have," says Maude Aimee. "There's a genuine love there, and if I needed prayer tomorrow or wanted somebody to help me with a burden, I would call Evelyn or Oral immediately." Maude Aimee is especially close to Richard Roberts, who now hosts his own Christian talk show at his father's television facilities. "Richard calls me his second mom. In fact on the phone the other day I said, 'Tell him it's his mom calling!' Richard asked, 'Which one?'"

A Best Friend: Kathryn Kuhlman

Of all the evangelists, Maude Aimee was closest to the late Kathryn Kuhlman. She has often called Kathryn her "dearest friend in the whole world." Located in Los Angeles, Miss Kuhlman was a well-known "faith-healer" noted for her flowing gowns and theatrical preaching style. She died in 1976.

Maude Aimee first met Kathryn in Akron, Ohio, when Kathryn asked Rex if she could use his Gospel Big Top for a Sunday service. "In those days, evangelists on the road were always borrowing from each other," remembers Maude Aimee. "One time we had bought a tent from Oral Roberts; then, a few months later, we sold it to Billy Graham."

On Saturday night, after the Humbards' service was over, Kathryn Kuhlman's crew went to work transforming the tent into a "thing of beauty." Kuhlman's service was scheduled to begin at eleven A.M. the next day, but at four in the morning the police came knocking at the Humbard trailer door. "Reverend Humbard, you're going to have to do something," said the policeman. "There's nearly eighteen thousand people out in your tent!"

Sure enough the six-thousand-seat tent was overflowing, and the eleven o'clock service had to start three hours early in order to accommodate the crowds. It continued that way Sunday after Sunday.

Along with all of the crowds came the first serious controversy in the ministry of Rex and Maude Aimee. Before Kathryn's arrival, the area churches encouraged attendance at the Humbard meetings. When Kathryn Kuhlman arrived, it all changed. Suddenly the churches felt threatened, and they forbade their congregations from attending the services.

Human nature being what it is, the forbidden became all the more tempting, and the Humbard meetings grew instead of shrank. But the controversy was not to end there. An Akron pastor, who opposed Kathryn's faith in healing, publicly challenged her in the city newspaper. He asked her to produce just one person that God had healed. If she could, he would give her five thousand dollars. Kathryn accepted the challenge on the stipulation the five thousand dollars would go to the United Fund.

Kathryn brought a prominent civic leader from Pittsburgh who had been healed of cancer. *Redbook* magazine had just completed a story on the man, and now here he was, ready to testify to the press. His story was published in the Akron *Beacon Journal,* and the newspaper's editor told the pastor to pay up. He never did. Instead, Kuhlman and the Humbards reaped the benefits of even more people attending their services.

During their stay of five weeks in Akron, the Humbards played host to more than two hundred thousand people, a record for such outdoor religious meetings. When the family moved on to Cleveland, Maude Aimee began to see many of the same faces she had come to recognize in Akron. Along with the memories, those faces strengthened Maude Aimee's fondness for Akron.

Rex felt the same way. "I had an experience and God spoke to my heart," says Rex. Soon Rex announced to his family, "I'm going to stay in Akron. I'm going to build a large church, go on television, go to every state in the union, and evangelize the whole world by electronics."

At this point the entire Humbard family had traveled and ministered together for a long time. Now Rex wanted to stay in Akron, but the remainder of his family wouldn't go along with him. "My dad wouldn't buy it, my brother wouldn't buy it, none of them. So the tent and my family left town after I traveled all those years with them. I had sixty-five dollars, a wife, and two small children. No church —nothing!"

Not quite "nothing"—he did have a large faith and a gift for preaching.

I think Rex Humbard is the greatest preacher alive, and I've heard them all. He has always been marked by two characteristics: a drive to give God his very best and a deep-rooted compassion for the lost. And that something deep down inside of Rex—that love for people—is what makes him great.

MAUDE AIMEE HUMBARD

Evangelist Rex Humbard was true to his commitment and his wife's faith in him. Within six years he built a large church. Within ten years he had taken the Gospel to every state in the United States. And by 1976 he indeed was involved in evangelizing the whole world by means of electronics.

EASTER IN AKRON

When Rex decided to remain in Akron, it was Maude Aimee's get-it-done personality that went to work. The Humbards' first church in Akron was Calvary Temple. Located in Cuyahoga Falls, a suburb of Akron, the church began at the Ohio State Theatre. Although it was a beautiful building, it still needed a great deal of work. That's where Maude Aimee took over.

"We were scheduled to open on Easter Sunday, April 5, 1953. I knew Rex couldn't hammer all day and then preach at night, so I sent him to Florida for a week to prepare himself." Clare Conlan, one of the trustees of the new church and an old family friend, offered Rex the use of his trailer in Pensacola. Rex gladly accepted.

Armed with a staff of volunteers and a vision of what the new church could be, Maude Aimee supervised the transformation. From Thursday night on, she never went to bed. When Rex first saw the finished church, he wept. Maude Aimee recalls, "It was an impossibility with man, but with God all things are possible." Perhaps with qualifications some members of the Humbard team might reword that statement to read: "It was an impossibility with man, but with Maude Aimee all things are possible."

That first service on Easter 1953 came about on a gray and overcast morning. Maude Aimee and Rex hoped for one thousand children in Sunday school. They beat that number by two. Within weeks more space was needed. They rented additional space for classes, and a short time later they leased yet another school building.

BUILDING A CATHEDRAL

While Calvary Temple was in its first few weeks of operation, Rex was planning something bigger. He had the idea of broadcasting on television to people all over the state. Within a year that dream had grown tenfold. They were broadcasting an early morning program live from Cleveland five days a week, an evening program in Akron, daily radio programs at nine-thirty A.M. and ten P.M., as well as an hour of recorded gospel music from twelve-thirty to one-thirty in the morning. Over one million people watched the Humbard meetings from six TV stations in Ohio, Pennsylvania, and West Virginia. And there was more.

The Humbard ministry also offered a four-hour prayer line, a "spiritual clinic" where people could meet with volunteer counselors, and there were twenty-two city buses that carried members to church each week. Less than a year after the opening of Calvary Temple, the congregation had outgrown the former Ohio State Theatre. They now needed a church five times larger than Calvary Temple's one-thousand-seat auditorium.

Rex and Maude Aimee found the perfect location soon after. It was only two miles from Calvary Temple, and again Maude Aimee led the way. It was there that Rex and Maude Aimee created their dream—the Cathedral of Tomorrow.

"Rex made himself general contractor and me his assistant," says Maude Aimee. "We didn't have a foreman on the job; I was it. Rex couldn't be there because he was still pastoring the church. I'd say, 'Come on, boys, let's get this done faster. We've got an opening date.' I climbed right up there with the boys laying the roof and checking it out to make sure it was just right. When it came time to paint it, I said, 'Come on boys, we've got to move faster than this. You're not working fast enough.'"

The workers would ask, "What do you want us to do, Mrs. Humbard, work night and day?" Matter of factly Maude Aimee would respond, "No, that's not fast enough. I want it done yesterday. That was my theme song, and still is today."

"Rex had the dream, and I made sure it came true," says Maude Aimee. That dream included a church like no other. It was round, on a single floor, with ramps for the handicapped and elderly. There would be a 165-foot hydraulically powered stage that would overlook five thousand seats. For a symbolic design Maude Aimee chose a blood-red curtain and red cushions on black-backed seats.

When you walk in, you see the red curtain and all the black backs of the chairs. When you get to the front and look to the rear, you see nothing but red. For Maude Aimee, the very colors of the sanctuary would remind the congregation of the blood of Christ.

Rex did design one key part of the building interior though. "He wanted the people to see something unusual when they came into the sanctuary, so when they left they would remember it as unique. He had the builders suspend a huge cross from the ceiling, with 4,500 lightbulbs of many different colors in it." For Maude Aimee that cross, suspended in the center of the auditorium, signified her and Rex's central theme: reaching the world with the Gospel. "That was Rex's dream," says Maude Aimee, "to fulfill the Great Commission literally—to go into all the world right there in Akron, Ohio, from that building."

REX HUMBARD: ELECTRONIC EVANGELIST

In 1970, the hour-long "Cathedral of Tomorrow" broadcast appeared on 242 stations, making it the number one evangelical television program in America. Sunday services began precisely at eleven A.M., with a song by the forty-eight-voice Cathedral Choir. Wayne Jones, the assistant pastor and Rex's brother-in-law, would then welcome the TV audience and introduce Rex. The evangelist then gave his message, aiming to reach "the masses, not the theologians." "We've got enough theology," he would often quip during the service. "What we need is more knee-ology."

At one time Rex had eleven ministers assisting him and a staff of 150 to handle the ministry. Two hundred thousand letters were sent monthly to the Humbards. On February 1, 1971, *The Wall Street Journal* ran a front-page story with the headline REX HUMBARD PREACHES OLD-FASHIONED RELIGION, USES MODERN METHODS. Four months later, *Time* magazine called him the "Electronic Evangelist." Rex didn't mind; in fact he was proud of himself. As Roman Catholic Cardinal Jamie L. Sin said, "If the Apostle Paul were alive today, he'd be using TV and radio just as Rex Humbard does."

An area Rex has always avoided is politics. He seldom speaks out on political or related controversial issues. "Jesus would never get into politics," says Rex Humbard. "We preach love out of the corners of our mouths, and then we jump on politicians. We should preach the Gospel to everybody."

Maude Aimee agrees. "You get a man's heart right or a woman's heart right, and you're not going to have problems. . . . You're going to do away with about five of the main issues in the newspapers today, even the federal budget problems." Rex is also careful not to tangle with the occasional heckler or critic. "My daddy always told me, 'If you want to smell like a polecat, fight one.'"

Death Knocks Twice

Throughout her life Maude Aimee always has been the fighter. In 1964 and again in July 1978 she faced her toughest struggles. She faced death head on.

The first encounter with death came two years after her youngest child Charley was born. Doctors told Maude Aimee she needed major surgery. For some reason she was sure it was the beginning of the end. She was so convinced of her imminent death that she arranged her own funeral. "When I went into surgery, I knew who I was, who I belonged to, and I knew where I was going. I was going to a place that I had preached about, that I sung about, that I've talked about."

The night before her surgery, a nurse came to check on Maude Aimee. The nurse could see that she was troubled, and so she advised her to read the 121st Psalm. It turned out to be good medical advice as Maude Aimee read:

> *I will lift up mine eyes unto the hills, from whence cometh my help. My help cometh from the Lord, which made heaven and earth. He will not suffer thy foot to be moved: he that keepeth thee will not slumber.*

Maude Aimee calls that nurse an "angel of mercy." That scripture turned her attitude around. She still felt some premonition, but somehow she knew everything would be alright.

The next morning at seven A.M., Maude Aimee was wheeled into the operating room. She warned the surgical team to be prepared. "We're going to have an accident here today. I'm either going to hemorrhage to death or my heart is going to stop." Just as Maude Aimee had predicted, as the surgery ended so did her heartbeat. The monitor went blank. The system's warning buzzer began to scream.

For five and a half hours, the doctors and nurses worked

on Mrs. Rex Humbard. She had lost pints of blood and in their attempt to replenish it, every vein punctured collapsed. They finally found a tiny vein in her hand that held. Still, by most medical standards, she should have already been dead.

Twelve hours after the operation, Maude Aimee was wheeled back into her hospital room. The doctor told Rex, "We saved her, but she's had all new blood. I don't know if her body will reject this blood or not. It's just touch and go."

That night Rex encouraged the congregation at the Cathedral of Tomorrow to pray for Maude Aimee. A week later her fever was gone and Maude Aimee was able to go home. Her recovery, however, was long and arduous, and Maude Aimee was overwhelmed by depression. As she was to recall later, "I heard the devil saying 'I missed her in surgery, but I have her now.'"

She refused to go to church. In the eleven months that followed, she only went twice. The criticism Maude Aimee had received in the past—about her singing, her clothes, the way she talked—now all these began to cause her pain and resentment. Yet even as people attacked her, others gave her support; and it was the latter who finally brought the evangelist's wife back to church again.

Fourteen years later Maude Aimee faced death a second time. She had a near fatal heart attack while in Brazil and clinically died on the operating table. After eight electric shocks, they finally revived her. "I remember coming to, and I hollered, 'My God, I don't want this! Where's Rex?' And I went out again and they brought me back with two more electric shocks. It just wasn't my time."

The Lord spoke to me during that time, and said, "Soldier, I have a job for you to do." I didn't see His face. I only saw that I was standing by Him in front of a calm lake. And there was a big white garment . . . but it was the words He said that I remember most. He could have said, "My child," but He said, "My soldier, I have a job for you to do."

MAUDE AIMEE HUMBARD

Today Maude Aimee almost jokes about her near brushes with death. Knowing what a survivor she is, Maude Aimee comically says, "I just know I'm going to be buried upside down, so if I dug out, I'd be digging down!" Still, she knows how she wants to be remembered. "I did the best I could, as honestly as I knew how. And I think the Lord would look down at me and say, 'Hey, I know just how you feel.'"

REX AND MAUDE AIMEE TODAY

Today the Rex Humbard family is as large as the family into which Maude Aimee married. Rex Jr. heads the operations of the ministry and Don handles the stewardship. Elizabeth oversees the writing and publications. Charley, after working as an audio technician, left to take a job with the Turner Broadcasting System. He was joined by Liz's husband, Dan.

Rex and Maude Aimee continue their ministry at an ever busy pace. Rex says, "I'll never retire, and I'll do my best as long as I can." Today he serves as Pastor Emeritus of the Cathedral of Tomorrow. According to Liz, her father felt badly about leaving the Sunday morning show, but had the knowledge that in other ways "he'd win more souls in his later years by reaching out again to the nonchurched."

The Humbards are also frequent guests on Jim and Tammy Bakker's "PTL Club" Show and maintain a close relationship with the Swaggarts. Elizabeth says, "Reverend Swaggart once said that in part God has used Rex to influence his ministry. Dad spoke to him in three ways. He inspired him to go into television, to do crusades, and to go international." Time has shown all three suggestions to be successful.

The greatest reward that Rex and I have had in our whole ministry is that our children have followed us in our work.

MAUDE AIMEE HUMBARD

After fifty-five years of ministry Maude Aimee and Rex's mission remains the same: to preach the Gospel. Above all else, says Rex, "We preach a theme that is universal. Christ is the answer in the United States, in Asia, in South America, in Africa, in every town, village, and region of the world."

Perhaps more than anything else, Maude Aimee knew it was Rex's destiny to preach that message. And it was her destiny to support him at every step and to assure that he met his call. "He saw the world as it is," writes Maude Aimee. "He walked the alleys as well as the main streets. And he grew into a product of the thousands of people he had seen and met, and the millions he would reach but never see. I never gave up because I know Rex is a man set apart. The destiny will not be denied. And his family has loved him and supported him all the more because of it."

EVELYN ROBERTS

❦

The Lord gave Oral the talent to do two things: the talent to preach and to love me.

EVELYN ROBERTS

On Sunday, February 27, 1977, like every other Sunday, thousands of television sets were being tuned to "Oral Roberts and You," Oral's half-hour Sunday morning broadcast. But today's program was not like every other Sunday. Just days before, Rebecca Roberts Nash, the thirty-seven-year-old daughter of Oral and Evelyn Roberts, and her husband Marshall Nash had been killed in a plane crash.

Phil Cooke, Director of Oral Roberts Television, recalls that show: "We were called at home when Marshall and Rebecca were killed. We were told that Oral wanted to come in and do a TV program. Of course Rebecca's death was the furthest thing from everyone's mind. As soon as Oral started talking into the camera, I realized that what they were doing was sharing their deepest hurt with the people who are closest to them—the partners in the ministry."

The show was very moving. There were Oral and Evelyn, holding hands and weeping. Oral did most of the talking, yet it was obvious that Evelyn shared his every thought. "It was probably as effective a program as any we've had," says Cooke, "simply because for one of the first times in history, two people willingly sat down at the lowest point of their lives and shared from their hearts. I think that really won a lot of people over, because they thought, 'If faith and God can get the Robertses through this, then maybe it will work for me.' " In fact, the broadcast that day became one of the highest-rated programs in all of Christian television.

LIFE FROM DEATH

The death of Rebecca could not have been more tragic or ironic. Evelyn does not like small airplanes. Shortly after Rebecca married, Evelyn advised her against a flight aboard a single-engine plane to join her husband. Rebecca heeded her mother's warning but later admitted that "it was the most miserable weekend" she had ever spent. "I would rather have gone with my husband and died than to have stayed at home alone," she told Evelyn. A year later her words proved to be prophetic.

On that February day in 1977, Rebecca and Marshall were returning to Tulsa, Oklahoma, after a skiing vacation in Aspen, Colorado. Flying in stormy weather, the plane crashed in Kansas. It was the "single worst day" in the life of Evelyn Roberts.

Oral alone decided to go before the TV cameras. "I can't just lay my hurt in front of everybody," Evelyn told Oral. "He said that if we don't do this, if we don't plant a seed of faith, this grief is going to kill us . . . and I couldn't let him go on and do it himself."

No one who watched that February 27 broadcast could be unmoved by the sight of the two grief-stricken parents, talking about the death of their daughter. Still, to Evelyn there was good that came from the tragedy. "It helped people to know that we were not up on a pedestal and never had grief. They cried with us and they prayed with us; they helped us get out of our grief."

After the tragedy of Rebecca's death, Evelyn went on to write two books on grief—a children's book, *Heaven Has a Floor,* and *Coping with Grief.* In her second book Evelyn writes, "God doesn't take our loved one away from us. God didn't take my daughter away from me. He accepted her." Such strong faith has been the message of Oral and Evelyn for almost fifty years. Yet behind those words Evelyn suffered. She especially remembers one night when she could no longer contain her sorrow.

> *I really lashed out at the Lord one night. I said, "Lord, you don't know what I've been through. You're not a mother and you just can't understand how a mother feels." And just as clear as I've ever heard anything, He said, "No, I've never been a mother and I don't know, but My mother knew, because she stood and watched Me die."*
>
> EVELYN ROBERTS

Evelyn's grief still continued. It was about six weeks after the plane crash, and as tears came to her eyes, Evelyn recalls, "I was getting sick in my body and I lost the joy out of my life. I said, 'Lord, what have I done to lose my joy?' He reminded me that music lifts me . . . suddenly I thought, you know, I haven't wanted to listen to any music since Rebecca died. And I just said, 'Satan, I will not let you have my joy.' The next morning I got up and I turned every piece of music on in the house and my joy came back."

A few days after the Sunday telecast on Rebecca's death, the Robertses went into seclusion in Palm Springs, California. From that experience came the most dramatic undertaking of the Oral Roberts ministry—the building of the City of Faith Medical and Research Center in Tulsa. "Richard, Oral, and I went out to the desert to just kind of get the cobwebs out of our minds and pull ourselves together . . . and the Lord began speaking to Oral. He gave him the blueprint right there for the City of Faith. It was because of the sudden deaths of Rebecca and Marshall that the City of Faith was built. It may never have been built if they had lived."

ANYONE BUT A PREACHER

Fifty years before dreams of hospitals and research centers there was just Oral and Evelyn—two young people with hope and faith and love.

Evelyn remembers that Oral "looked exactly like the person I had imagined marrying. I didn't know he was a minister or anything else about him. But I knew in my heart that he looked exactly like I wanted my husband to look." So sure was Evelyn of her feelings that she wrote in her diary, "Tonight I met my future husband. He is tall and handsome. Someday I intend to marry him."

As the stepdaughter of a devoted Pentecostal Christian, Evelyn was well prepared for the role of a minister's wife. Yet, like Macel Falwell and Frances Swaggart, she never intended to marry a preacher. She remembers a conversation with young Oral: "I told him I didn't want to marry a preacher, because most preachers I knew had a house full of children and that's all the wife could ever accomplish—to take care of those children. And I said, 'I won't be that kind of wife.' "

Evelyn knew too well the sacrifices which came with being a minister's wife. During the Depression her stepfather did some preaching, having been ordained in the Pentecostal Holiness Church. Evelyn and her sister Ruth traveled with him. Ruth played the violin while Evelyn played the guitar.

By the time Evelyn was ten, the family had settled down in Westville, Oklahoma, just across the Arkansas state line. Times were tough; Evelyn grew up in Depression poverty, as did many of the children in the area. Over the years Evelyn and Ruth were joined by six half-brothers and sisters—J.D., Kathleen, Betty, Paul, Bobbie, and George. As the eldest, Evelyn became the family baby-sitter whenever her parents attended one of the many revivals held in the area.

Evelyn was determined to break the cycle of poverty in her life. With some money she received from her maternal grandparents, she managed to attend Northeast State Teachers College in Tahlequah, Oklahoma. At the age of eighteen, she had earned her teaching certificate and was working in a one-room schoolhouse near Westville. Her pay was forty dollars a month, and with that she paid her parents' rent and bought their food.

Across the Hills

While Evelyn was struggling to help support her family, a young preacher by the name of Granville Oral Roberts was making a name for himself. Oral did not set out to be a preacher; it was his mother who helped convince him. As Evelyn recalls, "In the first place, preachers don't stutter or stammer, and Oral did, badly. In the second place, preachers were characteristically poor. Oral Roberts was sick and tired of being poor."

When Oral was fifteen, he set out to make some changes in his life. He left his home in Ada, Oklahoma, and moved in with a judge in Atoka. The judge gave Oral permission to read his law books. After reading them, Oral decided to study for a law career.

In high school Oral would do the chores in the judge's home, attend classes, practice basketball with the school team, deliver papers along his paper route, and then concentrate on his studies. On weekends he worked in a local grocery store and wrote a column for the Ada *Evening News*. Even in high school, Oral was intrigued with politics. He was class president and had set his sights on one day becoming governor of the state. Nothing was going to stand in his way, not even the demanding schedule he had set for himself.

All of Oral's hard work abruptly ended one night in February 1935. While playing in the final game of the Southern Oklahoma Basketball Tournament, he suddenly felt the life drain out of his lungs. He collapsed in a heap, bleeding from the mouth. His coach drove him to his family's home in Ada.

The diagnosis was tuberculosis in both lungs, and the disease was in its final stages. Oral's mother had lost her father and two older sisters to TB. It was a common-enough occurrence in the 1930s. For more than five months, Oral lay in bed, unable to talk and suffering with every breath. There was little hope that he would ever recover, until one day Oral's sister spoke seven words that would change Oral's life forever.

"Oral, God is going to heal you," said Oral's sister Jewel.

The words seemed simple enough. They seemed almost expected in the Roberts home. Yet they pierced Oral's fear and built his faith. With that spark of faith, Elmer, Oral's oldest brother, bundled up Oral for a trip to a revival meeting.

The evangelist who laid his hands on the seventeen-year-old Oral Roberts was Reverend George Moncey. Evelyn, who was to listen to the story many times over, later wrote, "Not only could he breathe, he could talk. He took deep breaths, going all the way to the bottom of his lungs without burning pain, coughing, or hemorrhaging. Then he took the microphone and walked up and down the platform telling people plainly what Jesus of Nazareth had done for him."

That July night in 1935 Oral received his healing; yet over and beyond that he received his call from God. It is a story that Oral and Evelyn have told thousands of times to millions of people. "Suddenly I was aware of God's presence," says Oral, and then in a voice that was "clear and unmistakable," Oral heard God tell him, "Son, I am going to heal you, and you are going to take My healing power to your generation."

A WEEKEND WITH A DECISION

By the summer of 1936, Oral had developed a strong following after he had started preaching that message. That popularity led Oral to the Sulphur, Oklahoma, camp meeting where he was to be licensed as a minister in the Pentecostal Holiness Church. It was a day he had eagerly anticipated for over a year. Although the young Oral had already enjoyed a degree of success as an evangelist, his ordination would be a "stamp of approval" on his ministry. It was that night in Sulphur when Oral and Evelyn first met. For now, though, the young evangelist wasn't looking for a wife; he was seeking a future.

It wasn't until two years later that Oral payed a formal "courting" visit to Evelyn down in Texas. In a previous letter, Oral had alluded to the idea that maybe the couple should spend the next fifty years together. Evelyn, who was determined not to marry a preacher, wrote back, calling Oral "presumptuous" and plainly telling him her thoughts on the idea. Now he had come calling, over four hundred miles from Oklahoma, with his mother in attendance.

The couple had one weekend together. They managed to fill it with picnics and long dinners and much conversation. Before Oral left for Oklahoma on Sunday evening, the two were engaged.

> *We've always had a good relationship—first of all, because we loved each other. God put us together. We really learned to love each other after we were married because we didn't have any courtship time.*
>
> EVELYN ROBERTS

Evelyn's teaching contract required that she remain unmarried, so they planned a June wedding after school had finished. But Oral, "being the hurry-up person that he is," campaigned for a Christmas wedding. Evelyn received special permission from the school board to marry in December, as long as she agreed to teach the remainder of the school year.

The wedding was scheduled, although Oral's finances were meager. To prepare for the wedding, Oral secured a twenty-dollar loan. The bank deducted two dollars for interest; three dollars went for flowers, five dollars for the minister; and with the remaining ten dollars, Oral headed for the church. The small wedding was held in Evelyn's hometown of Westville on Christmas Day, 1938, with the townspeople in attendance. As Evelyn was to write in her autobiography, "I married Oral Roberts on December 25, 1938, because I loved him and for no other reason."

UPS AND DOWNS OF THE MINISTRY

Evelyn vividly remembers the many turning points of Oral's early ministry. First was the launching of Oral's healing ministry with a meeting of 1,200 followers in downtown Enid, Oklahoma. A number of years later, while preaching in Tulsa, Oral was catapulted into national fame when a bullet from an angry protester ripped through Oral's tent canvas only eighteen inches from the evangelist's head.

Perhaps the most inspiring aspect of Oral's early ministry was his television show, where millions of Americans witnessed the drama of the healing line. The goal from the beginning was to re-create the atmosphere of the crusades on television. Every program featured a notary public, who would swear that the healings on camera did, in fact, take place.

During these and a myriad of other early events, it was Evelyn who held fast as Oral's strongest believer and closest adviser. She didn't take on the role of the "driven woman," as did Maude Aimee Humbard, but in other ways Evelyn assured her husband's success. Dr. John Messick, the first dean of Oral's university, wrote, "If it were not for her, I'm afraid Oral could not have succeeded to the extent he has. She's a *great lady.*"

Perhaps Evelyn's greatest contribution has been her un-yielding commitment to Oral and his message. As Evelyn often says, "My first duty is my husband. The Lord gave me my husband. He ministers to the people, so he has to have somebody to minister to him."

To understand how Evelyn "ministers to her husband," you first need an insight into the temperament of the couple. "Oral's always been a moody person," admits Evelyn. "He has ups and downs all the time. He's never level, but I am of German descent and I'm pretty stable all the way through." One of Oral's top executives, Dr. Jan Dargatz, agrees, saying, "When Oral gets down or gets sick, he . . . bottoms out, and he goes through intense grief. When he's high, he's higher than a kite and moving faster than any-body can move to catch up with him. Evelyn, on the other hand, is a person with a lot of routine in her life. She's a very orderly, even-tempered person."

> *Dad is up and down. He's a man with an imagination.*
> *Mostly he's up all the time with ideas running through*
> *his head twenty-four hours a day. Mother is not like that.*
> *She's very down to earth and very, very practical.*
> ROBERTA ROBERTS POTTS

How does Evelyn handle Oral's ups and downs? "Usually when he gets low, I'll take one of his sermons . . . on tape and set the tape in front of him and say, 'Look here. Listen to your own sermon. You tell other people it will bring them out. It will bring you out, too." Jan agrees that such a technique is effective, but it is only Oral's "darling wife Evelyn" who could bring it off.

By 1949 Oral had set a pattern for his ministry that would remain constant for the next decade. The "country's larg-est fireproof tent" moved from city to city and state to state.

The Roberts family now included four small children—Rebecca Ann, Ronald David, Richard Lee, and Roberta Jean. Evelyn remembers that time as "the most gratifying experience in the world. I just assumed that this was my time to be with my children and I was going to enjoy it as much as I could."

But like Billy and Ruth Graham, the life of Oral and Evelyn has been filled with long absences. More than all the other trips, Evelyn recalls taking Oral to the Tulsa airport for the flight to his first evangelistic crusade in the East. "My concern was being separated from Oral, the man I had married and wanted to be with for the rest of my life. It was a crisis time for me. . . ."

> *He kissed me good-bye, walked up the steps, and disappeared inside. Tears came to my eyes as I thought: Yes, good-bye, Oral. I'll probably be doing this the rest of my life. While we are both young, we should be together, but we have to be apart.*
>
> EVELYN ROBERTS

During his years of traveling, the loneliness of separation was as intensely felt by Oral. "There are times," recalls Oral, "I've called Evelyn to fly across the country to be by my side. I needed her. . . . it was because I become very lonely sometimes in my room, and I'm very much in love with my wife." Then there were times Evelyn simply went on her own, knowing that Oral couldn't stand to be by himself.

When Evelyn would arrive, Oral felt inspired: "It is a thrilling thing as I preach to look out and see her shining face. She loves to hear me preach and this inspires me to preach better." Once, when Evelyn was not in the audience, Oral began telling the congregation all about her. "I have a wonderful wife, Evelyn. Evelyn is getting prettier every day and sweeter every day. In fact, if I don't hush up, I won't even preach. I will get up and go home. I really love my wife."

PASS THE HAT PLEASE

Evelyn has always been Oral's closest adviser. "We sit down a lot of times before he preaches, and he'll ask me my opinion. . . . I am perfectly honest with him. He's open to my ideas." It's that honesty and openness which have held Oral and Evelyn so close. She once told a reporter, "We have never had secrets from each other. If he doesn't like something I do, he is quick to tell me he thinks it's wrong. I do the same."

During an early crusade, Evelyn did more than just pass advice to Oral, she went onto the platform and started to pass the hat. It was during one of those low points when Oral was ready to give up. The offering was almost barren. Oral felt if he couldn't trust God for finances, then he didn't have the right to preach. As he began to leave the stage, Evelyn walked onto the platform. "People, you don't know Oral like I do. He's not here for the money. He's here for the Gospel. . . . My husband's about to give up this ministry and I know he will do it. . . . I think you should do something about it." With that admonishment, Evelyn picked up a man's hat and took an offering. Never had she done such a thing—nor has she since. It's not "her style"; but that night it sure was needed.

By the early 1950s, the ministry of Oral Roberts extended beyond the boundaries of North America. In one year the evangelist traveled 250,000 miles, conducting more than 185 meetings. It seemed as if no country or village was immune to the word of Oral Roberts. A missionary once told him, "Oral, I once walked into a small hut out in the bush country: and your picture was hanging on the wall."

With the ministry growing by leaps and bounds, Evelyn's presence was needed more and more. It was not a role she particularly relished. In addition to her previous job as hat passer, she's often had the roles of chauffeur, office manager, mail sorter, and letter writer.

There have always been plenty of letters. Even today, Evelyn spends every day with the mail. According to daughter Roberta, "Evelyn works almost twenty-four hours a day, seven days a week. She answers a lot of letters from her bed. Even when she watches TV, she has her work in front of her. You wouldn't believe the things they write and some of the questions they ask," continues Roberta. For example, " 'I'm in this room and I've been locked up in here for six weeks—should I come out?' " A lot of people write that are lonely. They don't have anyone that cares about them and they are really reaching out."

TIME ALONE AND TIME TOGETHER

With Oral's growing worldwide ministry, Evelyn sometimes traveled with the healing teams and occasionally would join Oral on stage—but more often she stayed at home in Tulsa. Like Ruth Graham, Evelyn made her life out of her husband's absences.

The family life of Oral and Evelyn more and more revolved around Oral's brief visits home. She met him at the airport, often with children in tow, and she tried to make his few hours with her as special as possible. Fortunately all the time Oral was gone, nothing life-threatening happened to the children. She does recall one occasion when Roberta was sick and asked for her daddy. "Roberta was burning up with fever and hadn't slept all night. She said, 'If my daddy were here and prayed for me, I could go to sleep.' So I called Oral in the middle of the night. He talked to her and prayed over the telephone. It seemed to help her, just to hear her daddy's voice." Roberta went right to sleep after he prayed, and the next morning she was all right.

Another time when Oral was away, Evelyn was frightened by someone trying to break into the house. Evelyn was paralyzed with fear. She asked the Lord to let Oral know she was in trouble. A few minutes later, the intruder went away and Evelyn was able to return to sleep.

A few days later, she told Oral what had happened. "Evelyn, was this on Tuesday about three A.M.," Oral asked. Evelyn said yes, but how did he know? "He told me that at that exact hour someone awakened him and told him to get up. . . . A clear picture came to him of his children and me, and he saw us in danger." The next instant, Oral was on his knees, asking the Lord to protect his family. Evelyn was never again afraid during Oral's absences.

> *On one long overseas trip, Oral called and asked me to join him for the last week or so. Richard did not want me to go. When we returned, we discovered that Richard had taken his hatchet and chopped off his bedposts. When we asked him why, he said, "Well, Mother, I told you not to go overseas. And you went anyway, so I just thought, 'Okay, if Mother goes overseas, I'll just chop up my bed.'" And he did.*
>
> EVELYN ROBERTS

Evelyn's greatest joy during those years came from her children. Whenever possible, the children would join their father on stage, if only to lend some family support. Ronnie would sometimes sing, as did Richard, but the girls stayed more or less in the background. Evelyn sometimes yearns for those days. "I say to Oral sometimes, I wish I could have my little children around me, right now, for at least one day." There were struggles and hard times, but mostly there was laughter and great joy.

The pressure to raise the children "as normally as possible" also meant keeping the Roberts marriage "extraordinary." Oral once confided to Evelyn, "I don't want a normal marriage. If it can't be better than normal, then I don't want it. It has got to be above normal. I want us always to be sweethearts." Roberta recalls, "They've both worked at a good marriage . . . they are devoted to each other. Mom will arrange her schedule, or whatever she has to do, totally around him. And Dad depends on her. Dad can be thinking about some new mission and the men at the office will advise him, but then he'll come home and say, 'Evelyn, what do you think?' "

If Oral had his way, I would be sitting in his office every day through every conference he had all day long.

EVELYN ROBERTS

A CHRISTIAN BOOT CAMP

By 1960 Oral felt that the ministry was well on its way to bringing his healing message to the world. Now he was restless. He needed a new mission.

Since the time he had raised funds for Southwestern College in the 1940s, Oral had always been interested in higher education. In 1961 he envisioned a University of Evangelism to train American and foreign ministries. The idea started out as a sort of "boot camp" for budding evangelists and would become Oral's legacy to the world.

By 1965 the boot camp had become an accredited university, with an emphasis on high academic standards. Part of Oral's determination to see the university to fruition came from his deep concern for his son Ronnie, who had enrolled in Stanford University. "He went away to Stanford and started a different lifestyle than what he had at home," says Evelyn. Ronnie was majoring in foreign languages and was already fluent in German, French, and Chinese.

The pressures of being Oral Roberts's son and being exposed, for the first time, to the world of drugs eventually drove Ronnie to join the Army. Oral felt Ronnie's pain, and his urgency to build Oral Roberts University came partly from his desire to build a school for his own children.

Oral Roberts University, commonly referred to as ORU, was established in November 1962 and opened in the fall of

1965. The Reverend Billy Graham made the dedication speech, and the eyes of the world were once again on Oral Roberts.

The Roberts children were growing up quickly, though. About the same time that ORU was opening its doors, Roberta had turned fifteen, Richard was seventeen, and Ronnie had turned twenty-four. Rebecca, who was twenty-six, had already been married for seven years.

> *You can't tell your children that you love them too many times. We told ours that we loved them and we feel today we were a very affectionate family . . . we tell them, "You're so special in God's eyes because He just made one of you."*
>
> EVELYN ROBERTS

The teenage years were rebellious ones for the Roberts sons. First Ronnie, then Richard seemed to lash out against the rigid moral code that was a part of their lives. As a child, Ronnie enjoyed the crusades. When school permitted, he would often accompany his father to the meetings. In many ways, he was like Oral and, of all the children, seemed the most likely to follow in his father's footsteps.

But Ronnie had a dark side; a part of him resented the ministry that had deprived him of his father. School was almost a constant battle of defending his father, but Ronnie had a hard time communicating his pain. As Ronnie became a teenager and later a college student, he felt almost completely alienated from his father. By the time Ronnie had left Stanford and enlisted in the Army, he had started to abuse prescription drugs. He managed to hide his addiction from his parents for seventeen years. Evelyn says, "It was like he was not my son at all in those days. Oral and I had prayed with him and he had repented and he was all right in his spirit. But somehow or other, he just couldn't cope with life."

While Ronnie was silent about his dissatisfaction, Richard became vocal. Whenever Richard felt pushed to the limits, he would tell his father, "Leave me alone. Get off my back." For a time Richard was seen as the rebel in the family. Picking up some bad habits from a "fast-living" crowd, he smoked and often frequented nightclubs. He couldn't wait to get away from home and be off to college at Kansas University. Oral was devastated by Richard's decision not to attend ORU. Evelyn recalls, "He said to me, 'I've built a university and my own son doesn't even want to attend.'"

In time Richard did come to ORU. After spending a year at the University of Kansas Richard realized his father's university did have something to offer. He also faced the fact that he would have to make some drastic changes in his lifestyle to be accepted by the university. As Evelyn told him, "We are not going to make an exception, even for you."

The decision to attend ORU became a turning point in Richard's life. He began to attend crusades with his father and enjoyed singing with the ORU Collegians, later the World Action Singers. He met and married Patti Holcombe, an ORU student, and the couple began their own music ministry.

In comparison, Evelyn's daughters seemed to be content with their lives. Roberta recalls, "Dad didn't push us like he did the boys." Rebecca's only expression of defiance came when she dyed her naturally black hair blond. Roberta, as the youngest, reaped the benefits of her parents' "practicing" on the older children. As Evelyn wrote, "Having accepted Jesus into her heart at an early age, Roberta was really never rebellious." She loved the crusades and often played the piano and organ at the meetings.

SOMETHING GOOD IS ABOUT TO HAPPEN

By the end of the 1960s, Oral was wrestling with one more way to bring his message to the world. Having abandoned his old television series in 1965, he now felt the time was right for a new, more innovative approach to television evangelism. In March 1969 "Something Good Is Going to Happen to You" debuted on Sunday mornings. Gone were the healing lines and the testimonies—in their place were Hollywood personalities like Pat Boone and Anita Bryant. The stage was set for a new direction to Oral's ministry.

> *One of the most difficult things for me to do is to make television appearances. I'd much rather stand beside Oral with my faith and prayers and stand behind the camera while I'm praying. . . . It was never my desire to take part in the television ministry. I am not a public person. I don't have any desire to be.*
>
> EVELYN ROBERTS

Television director Phil Cooke agrees that Evelyn "doesn't relish being on camera. But when she's on, she's very experienced. She's very stable and consistent, and often gives a balance to the program that sometimes we don't otherwise have." More than balance, Evelyn provides a sense of upfront honesty. "She's very blunt with Oral," says Phil, "and I think viewers love that and respect it. On camera she talks with Oral quite comfortably. You almost get the feeling that she's in a kitchen talking to him over breakfast."

Television production is the one place in the Roberts ministry where Evelyn's presence is strongly felt—mostly indirectly. Phil admits that "Evelyn exerts a great amount of influence on the way we produce our TV program without ever saying a word. I've never been called up by Evelyn and chastised for one single frame . . . yet Evelyn is such an important figure that I can sense a certain direction from her in the way we shoot our programs."

In the early 1970s the Roberts television ministry was highlighted with spectacular prime-time specials. In 1972 there was a dramatic presentation of the Crucifixion, starring Peter Graves as Luke, Jane Powell as Pilate's wife, and Harvey Presnell as a Roman centurion. Such shows received critical acclaim and three Emmy nominations in 1971.

Both Oral and Evelyn later admitted that their new "star-studded" approach to television made them uneasy. Initial response to the new programming was negative; partners wrote in saying that they felt Oral Roberts had "gone Hollywood."

A few months later the tide turned and the "Oral Roberts Specials" began to earn strong ratings. By the end of the first year, the mail was running a thousand to one in favor of the programs. Meanwhile the number of student inquiries to the university had doubled. Old friend Rex Humbard commented at the time, "Oral Roberts is reaching more nonchurch people than any man in America, because he has taken a new approach and he's not afraid of criticism of church people."

A NEW METHOD FOR THE ROBERTSES

During this time while the university was growing and the television ministry was expanding, an important change was taking place in the Robertses' lives. In 1968 Oral and Evelyn changed churches. They left the Pentecostal Holiness Church and joined the Methodist denomination. It was a decision that had been a long time in coming. As early as 1947 Oral had been considering joining the Methodist Church. When he and Evelyn did finally make the change, it was without any fanfare. A person's decision to change churches was, to Oral and Evelyn, a very private affair.

Oral's decision was rooted in his desire to preach more freely. During his early days as a Pentecostal Holiness minister, he often butted heads with church leaders. When the decision to change churches was finally made, Oral was quick to point out that he wasn't changing his ministry; he was only changing his pulpit.

The news, however, soon spread, and almost overnight the ministry lost half its members. The ministry's mail began to contain letters full of anger and hurt. When Oral was ordained an elder in the church, he and Evelyn came under strong attack by headstrong Pentecostals. Evelyn recalls, "I'm not denying that negative letters and loss of partners hurt us. They did, deeply." Slowly the invitations from Methodist conferences and meetings came in, accepting the Robertses as brethren. He soon regained his lost members and then some.

A QUESTION OF WHY

In 1977 Evelyn was grieving over the recent loss of her daughter Rebecca, and at about the same time, her son Ronnie was headed down a path of self-destruction.

During his tour with the Army, Ronnie continued to abuse drugs. Evelyn explains, "He never stuck a needle in his arm or anything like that . . . but he was taking prescription drugs." When Carol, Ronnie's wife, discovered her husband was abusing drugs, she divorced him. "His life just went downhill after that and he just couldn't cope with life," says Evelyn. On June 9, 1982, Ronnie apparently became the victim of a self-inflicted gunshot wound. In a note he had written, Ronnie said, among other things, that he looked forward to seeing his sister Rebecca again. Roberta said, "It was as if Rebecca had died all over again."

Four hours after Ronnie's death, Oral took some notes about his feelings. He later expanded them into an article for *Christianity Today* magazine. Drugs were the "beginning of the end," for Ronnie, wrote Oral. He recalls times when Ronnie would visit "when he was not normal." Oral and Evelyn had reached out to their troubled son—but he couldn't and didn't accept their help.

For Evelyn the hardest part of Ronnie's death to accept was the fact that it was a suicide. She had been taught that "if you committed suicide, you went straight to hell."

"Where is the Scripture that says if you take your own life, you'll go to hell?" asked Evelyn. A friend told her, "There is nothing in the Bible like that." Evelyn later found comfort in the book of Corinthians, a verse explaining that the Lord turns the flesh of a person over to the devil so the spirit can be saved. "See, the last enemy of man is flesh. And the devil has power over that. So the Lord just let the devil have Ronnie's flesh so that his spirit could be saved."

Since their deaths, Evelyn admits she has seen both Rebecca and Ronnie in her dreams and "Every time she appears, she's so happy that I wouldn't take her away from where she is for anything." Of Ronnie, she says, "Right after he died, I kept saying, 'Lord, let me see him in my dreams like I see Rebecca, because she's happy and I want to know if he's all right, too.' " It was Oral who first saw Ronnie in his dreams. "One morning he came to the breakfast table and he said, 'Last night I saw Ronnie in my dreams . . . he was standing in a group with my mother, Rebecca, and Jesus. Ronnie was talking to Jesus and they were all smiling.' And Ronnie said, 'Lord, I am so grateful to be free of a body out of control.' "

Today Evelyn warns parents to be on the alert to the dangers of drugs. "I think parents should be very careful to watch the actions of a child. Watch and see if their behavior changes. And pray with them everyday before they go out the door for the Lord to protect them." She says it's a different generation today and "you have to do things nowadays that maybe we didn't have to do when our children were growing up."

PASSING THE MANTLE

Ask Oral Roberts what he believes to be his greatest accomplishment, and he will answer, "The healing lines." "Everything I've done, with the grace of God, began with my healing," he once told Evelyn. "And it's multiplied a thousandfold since."

When Oral leaves this earth, he will be known for two things—his healing ministry and his faith. He opened up healing in this country at a time when people thought the day of healing was over.

EVELYN ROBERTS

A key part of Oral's healing ministry is the City of Faith and its School of Medicine. Though it has been the subject of much controversy and has struggled financially, today this healing center includes three towers: the twenty-story research center; a sixty-story outpatient clinic; and a thirty-story hospital. Partners from Oral Roberts's worldwide ministry travel to Tulsa to receive prayer and be treated by some of the foremost medical professionals in the country here. Evelyn says, "When I see the City of Faith, I see Rebecca, because it was out of her death that so many are able to live."

In the 1980s son Richard is the second integral part of the Oral Roberts ministry. With a ministry and TV show of his own, Richard Roberts continues to spread his father's healing message. "The good part," says Evelyn, "is we're getting in these new partners now, from Richard's ministry. . . . See, Oral was Richard's age when we attracted all these partners that have been with us for thirty years. Now their children are accepting Richard . . . and when we're gone, they'll just go right along with Richard and the ministry will flow just like it's flowing now."

Because Richard is the apparent heir to the leadership of the Oral Roberts Evangelistic Association, his life has come under close scrutiny. Partners were especially disappointed by his divorce from Patti Holcombe, the young singer he had dated during the television years. Richard himself took the collapse of his marriage in 1979 as a personal failure. Still, Richard's call to preach received the complete support of the Oral Roberts ministry, and indeed, by 1982, the organization had redirected its energies toward Richard

Roberts. His crusades became the primary evangelistic thrust of the ministry for the 1980s.

In 1980 Richard was remarried to Lindsay Ann Salem, an ORU law student, who today cohosts "The Richard Roberts Show." While some insiders questioned the marriage so soon after Richard's divorce, the family and partners came to embrace Lindsay as their own.

The year 1984 brought yet another tragedy to the Roberts family. Richard Oral Roberts, born January 17 to Richard and Lindsay, died just a few hours after his birth. The death of his namesake hit Oral particularly hard. "It hurt him as much as losing one of his own children," admitted Evelyn.

Such common sorrows seemed to always bring Oral and Evelyn even closer. After forty-eight years of marriage, Oral still unabashedly adores his wife. Evelyn comments, "He told me not long ago, 'I have to honestly say to you, I have never seen another woman that I have wanted since I met you.'" The same devotion is also characteristic of Evelyn. Cheryl Prewitt Salem, Miss America of 1980 and a featured singer on "The Richard Roberts Show," says, "God could not have chosen a more perfect woman for Oral Roberts. She makes his strengths shine and if there is ever a slight weakness in Oral, she makes up the difference. . . ."

Now, as the couple enter their fifth decade as man and wife, Evelyn is looking forward to more time alone with Oral. She considers every day with him "a blessing." "I am in perfect health," she confides happily, "and I just thank the Lord every day for good health."

Across the nation and around the world there are millions who can be thankful for the "good health" Oral Roberts helped bring them—health for their body and soul, through his praying hands and the faith he built in them. Millions will remember the outstretched hands of Oral and the drama of the healing lines. Millions of others will remember the intensity of Oral through television. As Phil

Cooke said, "The magic of Oral Roberts is the magic of the close-up. He has a great spiritual and emotional impact . . . and you feel that he's right there in your home with you."

"The whole thesis of the ministry," says Evelyn, "is that God is a good God." For Evelyn and Oral, that includes a God for two lost children and a grandchild, and a God for the healing of sickness, poverty, depression, and all of life's ills. For the next ten years, Oral and Evelyn will concentrate on spreading that good news through healing teams overseas. "That's our big project now and probably will be as long as we have life in our bodies," says Evelyn.

Will they ever quit? "I'll quit when Oral quits," says Evelyn. "Never."

ARVELLA SCHULLER

> *I have always loved music, and had planned to become a professional musician. But I met the man who is my husband. "Marry me now," he proposed, "and finish your music studies later." Love won out! There has never been a doubt in my mind. I know I made the right choice.*
>
> ARVELLA SCHULLER

Choices and decisions—they have always formed the cross-roads of life. For Arvella Schuller these crossroads began among the rolling hills of northwestern Iowa and led her to the endless summers of Southern California. Along the way, Arvella's motto has always been the same: "Decide with your head, and your heart will follow! Our children have heard this principle preached, explained, visualized, and dramatized."

For Arvella, the choice when "love won out" was one of the most important in her life. The year was 1950, and a promising seminary student by the name of Robert Schuller was about to graduate from Western Theological Seminary. He was soon to start his first pastorate at Ivanhoe Reformed Church in a suburb of Riverdale, Illinois, on the far South Side of Chicago.

It wasn't a prestigious assignment. The congregation had dwindled to fewer than forty members. But young Robert Schuller wasn't seeking prestige; he was seeking a challenge. He was also looking for someone to help him meet that challenge. He would find his ultimate challenge in Southern California, later. He found his partner in a young farmer's daughter, Arvella DeHaan.

A Musical Beginning

Robert Schuller and Arvella DeHaan both grew up in tiny Newkirk, Iowa. It was a typical Iowa farming town, with a general store on one corner, a church on the next, a school on the third, and an almost never-ending cornfield on the fourth. In 1943 Newkirk High had all of seventy-four students, with Arvella entering as a freshman and Robert leaving as a senior. With four years separating them, the two didn't meet until five years later.

Like her husband, Arvella's family struggled to make ends meet on the farm. "We had a large family; we had very little money, so we had plenty of hand-me-downs. And we had to work, too. I had to drop out of school after the eighth grade for one year. I didn't think I would ever go back, because my mother was so ill. I did all the wash, the laundry, and the cooking for the family. This meant carrying water a long distance out of a well and heating it on a stove. There was nine of us counting Mom and Dad. What I remember about that year was not all of the hard work—that didn't bother me—but the thought that maybe I would never be able to go back to school to continue my music."

It was Arvella's music that eventually brought the Schullers together. Young Robert Schuller returned to Newkirk for the summer of 1948 as a visiting minister. One day, as Arvella sat practicing at the church organ, the doors of the church swung open and in walked the young minister. He was taken with the enchanting music and the attractive young woman who was creating it. He said nothing, but silently stood and listened.

Robert finally approached the young organist, saying, "Hi there."

"Oh, you startled me."

"I'm sorry," he quickly replied, "I guess you didn't hear me come in. You were pretty involved. That must be why you play so beautifully. Let me introduce myself. I'm Robert Schuller, the visiting minister here this week. And you must be Arvella."

"Yes," she answered shyly. "I suppose you want to discuss the hymns for this Sunday."

That was exactly why the young seminary student had come searching for the organist of the Newkirk Reformed Church. However, Robert now found it difficult to concentrate on church hymns. Arvella captivated him, and within hours his decision was made: Arvella was the one girl for him. In fact, after their first date, he wrote his best friend: "Bill, I've met the girl I'm going to marry."

ENDLESS ROMANCE

Music and romance have always been a part of Arvella's life. Early in their marriage, Robert bought a two-manual organ especially for Arvella to use during the services. With a gift of four hundred dollars he made the down payment; his four-thousand-dollar yearly salary barely stretched to make the remaining monthy payments of thirty-eight dollars. Their only son, Robert Anthony, explains, "They didn't have one extra nickel to spend in those days, but they were completely committed to their goal and crazy in love."

Even today, with the newlywed's gleam still in her eyes, Arvella admits that "we're still crazy in love. I have a marvelous husband who tells me every day that I am beautiful. He tells me this when he's in bed with his glasses off. I know he can't see without his glasses. Nevertheless, I love to hear it anyway."

Our individual roles were neatly kept in two boxes, one marked "his" and the other marked "hers." Now, thirty years later, the two boxes have become one circle of responsibility tied with a ribbon of love.

ARVELLA SCHULLER

The Schullers' third daughter, Carol, feels her parents' continuing romance is the one thing that would most surprise people. "They're very romantic. I always hear Dad comment on how beautiful Mom is. He'll go up and tell her, and then kiss her. She'll start smiling. They're just real romantic."

For Arvella, one of the keys to an enduring romance is "Never stop dating each other!" After six years of marriage Robert and Arvella discovered there was no private time just for the two of them. It was the summer of 1956, and a couple of college coeds had joined the Schullers for a few weeks. The result was six people living in a tiny house. To get away from the crowd, Robert asked out Arvella for a date.

When everyone asked what the occasion was, he simply responded, "I need to talk quietly with my wife. I love you all, but I love her more and want to spend a quiet evening alone with her."

Both Robert and Arvella enjoyed their "date" so much that they decided to make it a regular event on their calendar. Now, as the Schullers plan their next year's activities, Arvella takes her pen and each week writes in "time for love"—their date night.

When the Schuller children were growing up, date night was Monday evening. "We knew, as children, that Monday night was the night you didn't expect Mom and Dad to be with you," explains Carol, "unless it was something special. They usually got dressed up and would go out to dinner."

"First we talk shop," says Arvella, "often planning schedules for the family. We have discussed our budget and cash flow. We even get into deep philosophical discussions. . . .

Sometimes we talk with such intensity that we are unaware of others watching us. . . . Our weekly night out allows us to begin to know each other with a greater depth of understanding."

In the last few years these dates have expanded to include afternoons. "Often they'll leave about twelve noon from the office and go down to the beach to spend the day together," says Carol. "They'll come home after ten or eleven at night."

ONLY IN CALIFORNIA

After living in Illinois for five years, Robert and Arvella Schuller accepted an invitation from their denomination to move to California. They weren't, however, moving to a larger, more established church. They had accepted a call to start a "mission church" in Garden Grove. It was a "church" with no members, no building, no office, nothing —it was only a dream. Arvella recalls, "I had to trust in my husband when he came to California. I had never been here before. Just to follow him and remain believing in him was difficult."

> *My mom has said that she would never dare to do a lot of the things that my dad would do. She's not as "chancy." She loves that part of Dad. She would have stayed in a town in Iowa. She was scared to come out here to California. My dad is much more adventurous and I think she likes that in him.*
>
> CAROL SCHULLER

Just before the Schullers left Illinois, a denominational representative called on them to explain that there was no available meeting place for the new church. The message was straightforward: "It's simply impossible to find a hall to rent."

By now, "impossible" was a word Robert Schuller had

removed from his vocabulary. While stopping for lunch in an Albuquerque, New Mexico, coffee shop, he took a pen from his pocket and began to brainstorm. Quickly he wrote down ten ideas for a meeting place. The last was "rent a drive-in theater." And that's what he did.

Southern California's first drive-in church was scheduled to open on March 27, 1955. Years later, in a Los Angeles *Times* interview, Arvella recalls that first service. "There was no stained-glass window, no gold cross, no props. Just a microphone and Bob standing alone on a sticky tar-paper roof. He had to dip into his own imagination and become an entertainer and an inspirer. Call it theatrical presence and you won't be far wrong."

After a year and a half of this outdoor ministry, Robert Schuller decided the church needed a permanent structure. On September 23, 1956, the new permanent home of Garden Grove Community Church held its first service. The Rev. Dr. Schuller held the nine-thirty service at the small chapel on the corner of Chapman and Seacrest, then dashed for the Orange Drive-In Theater for the eleven o'clock outdoor service.

For four years the young pastor kept up this hectic schedule with two sanctuaries. In 1960 the congregation numbered more than seven hundred, and Robert and Arvella felt it was time to combine the two services into one walk-in/drive-in church. "It was a big positive step at the risk of a tremendous amount of criticism from his denomination, which is very austere, traditional, and conservative," says Arvella. "They were embarrassed with him being in a drive-in and now they thought, 'What's this Schuller going to do with a walk-in/drive-in church?' That was our most difficult period—the two years when his motives were questioned."

Regardless of the criticism, the Schullers pushed ahead with their building plans. In November 1961 Dr. Norman Vincent Peale dedicated the innovative structure—the new thousand-seat Garden Grove Community Church.

*If you're not being criticized, then you'd better examine
what you're doing—because you probably aren't doing
much or you're not daring to step out beyond the ordinary.*

ARVELLA SCHULLER

TOGETHER A GREAT TEAM

During all the planning, building, and possibility thinking, both in Illinois and California, Robert and Arvella
Schuller have always worked side by side. " 'Together we
make a great team' is our career slogan," says Arvella.
Marge Kelley, Dr. Schuller's secretary, adds, "They're definitely a team. He simply could not have done it without her.
He's the first one to say this. One thing I admire about him
is that he never hesitates, never loses an opportunity to give
her the credit that's due her."

*She's the earthy part of the twosome. Whatever God for-
got to put in him he put in her. The blend is fantastic. Just
for God to have put those two together in a little town in
Iowa, that is miraculous in itself.*

TRUDI AMERIKHANIAN

The key to the Schuller team success is their complemen-
tary personalities. "Both are geniuses," says Marge Kelley,
and both are perfectionists in everything. They're detail
people. Robert is the dreamer, the innovator, the orator,
while Arvella is the planner and the architect. According to
the Reverend Coffin, an early associate minister, Robert
Schuller has the ability to develop "great ideas and move
on them swiftly. He is more impulsive, and of course that's
the greatness of the man. Arvella is a calming influence,
more deliberate, not as impulsive."

Like the Robertses in Tulsa, the difference between
Arvella and her husband is primarily one of mood and
temperament. According to Dr. Schuller's secretary, "when
you talk of Oral and Evelyn Roberts . . . there is certainly

the same story here. His personality is changeable and he sees all the possibilities. He's willing to go in every direction, all at the same time." In contrast, "Arvella has her two feet solidly on the ground," says Dr. Norman Vincent Peale's wife, Ruth. "When Bob goes off to the clouds thinking and creating, Arvella is still there looking at every angle of what's being planned."

> *She's like a block of granite. I think that she can be immovable at times, in terms of standing up for what she thinks is right.*
>
> MARGE KELLEY

Arvella also has part of Maude Aimee Humbard's driven personality. While daughter Carol feels most people would be surprised at the Schullers' lifelong romance, a top "Hour of Power" executive offers a second surprise. For him, most viewers are totally unaware of Arvella's personal strength. "Behind the scenes, Arvella is as *strong* a person as you would *ever* hope to deal with." Yet, unlike Maude Aimee "I don't think she's aware of it."

> *She seems so disarming, so relaxed, and so friendly. I think people would be shocked to know the very keen understanding of marketing, figures, and money which she has.*
>
> JIM COLEMAN, PRESIDENT,
> "The Hour of Power"

From where did Arvella gain her personal strength? Ministry Associate Trudi Amerikhanian attributes it to Arvella's Dutch background. "I'm also a Dutch girl, reared in a Dutch home, with parents who came from the Netherlands about the same time. That's where the commitment was learned, that's where the hard stuff was learned. You have to look at the Dutch people. They say that God created the world, but the Dutch people created Holland; they moved back the waters. They had a tremendous 'stick-to-itive-ness.' "

As one who works with Arvella on a regular basis, Trudi adds that Arvella makes her feel "that I can do anything. She has a wonderful ability to build confidence, to help you believe in yourself. When the going gets tough, that's when Arvella starts to laugh. She laughs a lot. When I'm against the wall, I say, 'Arvella, what are we going to do?' and she'll start to laugh. . . ." When the laughter stops, that's when Arvella's Dutch determination begins.

THE CRYSTAL CATHEDRAL

Between 1960 and 1970 the congregation of the Garden Grove Community Church grew from seven hundred to more than five thousand. Robert Schuller decided it was time to take up another challenge. When completed, this challenge would be the greatest accomplishment of Robert and Arvella Schuller's ministry. It would be called the Crystal Cathedral.

In the mid-1970s the Schullers began a concentrated search for the cathedral's architect. It was Arvella who, on a transcontinental plane flight, found their answer while leafing through a *Vogue* magazine. The architect was Philip Johnson, and in the magazine Arvella saw his captivating "Water Gardens in Fort Worth." Soon Mr. Johnson was part of the Schuller team.

If finding an architect was an easy task, completing the cathedral wasn't. There were countless setbacks caused by foul weather, financial difficulties, and construction complexities. Finally, after five years of uphill struggle, the Crystal Cathedral was dedicated on September 14, 1980. Today the cathedral stands as a tribute to modern architecture and the Schullers' positive faith. The structure includes 10,661 silver mirrored windows, each six feet tall by two feet wide, and a Fratelli-Ruffatti organ with more than six thousand pipes. Because of the immensity of the sanctuary, a recent addition has been a fourteen-by-eighteen-foot Sony screen, similar to those used at professional sports arenas. The screen allows the congregation to enjoy close-up views of the speaker and other platform guests.

"THE HOUR OF POWER"

For the last seventeen years the Schullers' television ministry, "The Hour of Power," has grown in viewing audience and impact along with the church membership and the new structures. Started in 1970 with pledges of more than $200,000, within a decade the broadcast would be viewed in 176 cities in the United States, in addition to Canada and Australia. As "The Hour of Power" evolved, so did Arvella's participation in it. Today she is the Executive Producer.

"I was always in the music area of the church," says Arvella. "I knew worship; I didn't know television. My husband just said to me, 'Honey, I need you because I'm still a pastor . . . and I have my message each week. Would you take over the rest of the program? You know worship, you know me, you know our people and our audience.' I said, 'I don't know anything about television.' He replied, 'No, but you can learn.' "

> *She really is the architect of the "Hour of Power" television program. She does a beautiful job in putting that broadcast together. It's an expression from behind the scenes of her whole concept of worship and ministry.*
>
> MRS. JEAN COFFINS

Since she is the Executive Producer, the "overall look and feel of 'The Hour of Power' is Arvella's," explains producer-director Phil Kolbo. "We know that we are the only church on television, the true full church service, from beginning to end. Arvella's main responsibility is to make it a church service . . . for the congregation, and our congregation . . . is a viewing audience of over five million people."

Before any of those five million viewers enjoy "The Hour of Power," Arvella and her staff go through months of work and preparation. Two or three months before a particular Sunday, Arvella and her oldest daughter, Sheila, select that week's Scripture readings, music, and prayers. The goal is to coordinate the service around one central theme. During the last two years those themes have centered on chapters of Robert Schuller's bestselling books.

With the theme and program details chosen, one of Arvella's assistants works to see which artists, such as professional singers or speakers, are available for the service. After the artists are selected, the twenty-five-member production staff meets on Thursday of each week to review in detail the content of the broadcast. During this meeting the production staff listens to all the music and decides on the staging. That evening a full rehearsal is conducted in the Crystal Cathedral. In attendance are the choir, sometimes the featured soloist, and always the television director, who decides on the camera positions and other technical details for the taping three days later.

On Friday morning everything is refined and polished; on Saturday, nothing is done. On Sunday morning, however, everyone gets an early start. At 4:30 A.M. the rented television equipment is unloaded into the cathedral and moved into place. At five the production team is ready to rehearse the service. By nine-thirty the sanctuary is full and everything is ready to go.

The service is soon under way, and while Dr. Robert Schuller is preaching, Arvella is sitting downstairs in the executive broadcast room. Although much of the work is over, Arvella the perfectionist is still concerned with the service. A humorous anecdote illustrates the point.

Once, in the middle of Dr. Schuller's message, the pulpit phone rang. Phil Kolbo explains, "Robert picked it up, then put it back down and made the comment to the congregation that everything was going fine. He just got a call from the 'man' upstairs." Actually the call and the okay came from Arvella, who was sitting twenty-five feet below him in the cathedral broadcast center.

The televison broadcast center consists of three small rooms joined by glass walls and doors. It's actually quite confining. During a service Arvella normally remains in the viewing area, while the technical director and his assistants sit in the control room. At any time Arvella has her choice of viewing any of six monitors. The monitors have been given such names as First Mark, Paul, and Third John, as well as "jumbotron" for the large Sony screen located for all to view close-ups as they sit in the Crystal Cathedral sanctuary.

On the Monday morning after the service, Arvella and her associate producers begin editing the program. Their work will take them through Thursday morning. It's then time for another production meeting, and the entire cycle is repeated. When completed, the master tape is reproduced, and separate tapes are sent across the country and around the world. Of course, all of this takes time, and the final program viewers enjoy was usually taped three weeks earlier.

> *Basically, what we're doing is producing thirty-five specials a year. We do a special in three weeks, which is almost unheard-of. In all, we produce enough shows to fill out fifty-two weeks.*
>
> PHIL KOLBO

While the "glamour work" takes place in the Crystal Cathedral, the daily "nuts and bolts" of the ministry are located across the street in the "Hour of Power" building. One of the Schullers' three sons-in-law holds the title of President of "The Hour of Power," yet Arvella is still deeply involved in almost all aspects of the operation. "Every part of the ministry demands something from her," says

Phil Kolbo. "She feels every part of the ministry; and she gives to every part. It's amazing. I see her schedule sometimes, and I really don't know how she does it. She's just totally involved in what goes on."

Part of that work includes helping her husband with writing and preparing his books. In recent years, Arvella has assisted Robert through rewriting and editing. "She's edited the last two or three books and has done very well," says Marge Kelley. "Actually, they're his bestsellers."

A Role Model: Mrs. Norman Vincent Peale

The skills Arvella uses to make "The Hour of Power" successful are the same skills she counted on while raising her family. Again, Arvella uses a "team approach." "I first learned of team marriages as I watched my mother team up with Dad in the struggle to succeed on the farm in northwest Iowa. Two minds are better than one. Great accomplishments are completed by teams."

Two of the most important lessons Arvella has learned in life concern her family. The first came after six years of marriage. "I finally recognized there was a difference between a positive and negative faith. I was raised in a Christian home and made my commitment at the age of sixteen . . . yet I didn't realize there was a negative and a positive way in which to live."

In detail Arvella recalls that lesson: "The office was in our home. Meetings were taking place in the living room, and I was handing out sandwiches. Someone was knocking at the door and crying; and meanwhile the babies had to be diapered, the telephone was ringing . . . I just couldn't cope. I then began to realize that my husband's positive messages were meant for me. They weren't meant just for the pulpit, they were something that would work for me in my everyday nitty-gritty part of life. I began from that day on to read my Bible, especially the positive parts, and underline them. If it hadn't been for that, I don't think our family—or the ministry—would be what it is today."

> *The basic problem with the American family today is that . . . we've stopped looking! We've stopped talking! We've stopped touching! If we are to heal the hurts of the nation, let's begin with the family.*
>
> ARVELLA SCHULLER

The second lesson Arvella learned was from Mrs. Norman Vincent Peale. Arvella had long admired Dr. and Mrs. Peale and their positive faith. When Arvella was about to meet the wife of this famous Christian leader, she felt awestruck in her presence. Finally, after a few nervous moments, Arvella asked, "Mrs. Peale, what are your latest and newest projects?"

"I shall never forget her long pause and the way she looked me directly in the eye. I knew she strongly believed in whatever she was about to say," writes Arvella. " 'I have only one project,' she said confidently, 'and *He* is my *Husband!*' "

Mrs. Peale's statement became a turning point for Arvella. "From that time to this, I rearranged my priorities as follows: husband first; children second; career third; music fourth; volunteer organizations fifth. If you would ask my husband today, he would say my family is more important than my ministry. Because what good do we do for God . . . or for our nation . . . if our family goes to pieces? So we put each other first. Robert and I have our date night once a week, and then we have our date day with our children."

Arvella's children have always been the joy of her life. "What a pleasure my family has been to me throughout these thirty mothering years. Sitting in a big chair and holding them in my arms, or now that they are too big to snuggle on my lap, sitting beside them on the couch or around our dinner table with them, is one of the greatest pleasures of my life."

Yet, like Macel Falwell, Arvella knew little about children when she got married. With little money and less knowledge of caring for a newborn, "we became the scared parents of our very own first baby." Yet "if I was scared, my husband was terrified." After a shaky start, the Schuller family eventually included five children—Sheila Louise, Robert Anthony, Jeanne Ann, Carol Lynn, and Gretchen Joy.

During the many years raising five children, Arvella and her husband used all their talents to give them a positive faith. In her book *The Positive Family*, Arvella writes that a family is "a cluster in which each member is a builder of another, for the I AM must precede the I CAN. Some men build bridges, other tall skyscrapers—but a mother builds a leader for tomorrow's world."

> *We will not quit on each other. We as a family, can solve any* problem! *Meet any crisis! No matter how great! We, as a family, will stick together!*
>
> ARVELLA SCHULLER

THE SEX-SUCCESSFUL MARRIAGE

After thirty years of marriage, Arvella is sharing what she has learned in seminars entitled "Celebration of Marriage." As the title suggests, these conferences are not a clinic for troubled couples; rather, they are a time to reflect on the joys of marriage and help couples set new goals.

The workshop discusses all the different aspects of marriage. In keeping with her husband's thoughts on possibility thinking and creativity, one innovative idea Arvella shares with her participants is "sexual experience can release creative ideas."

"God created sex and ordained it, with a Christian husband and wife in the marriage setting. I think God has designed it to be the important part of creativity. I believe it very strongly. First to create a new life in a form of a baby, but also that we are more creative when we enjoy sex with each other because it just releases you."

Arvella is quick to add that "marriage isn't just a physical thing, but it begins there. It then develops and grows into a social and spiritual oneness. So it isn't just sex, that's only the beginning. If you're not talking in the kitchen and enjoying each other and communicating, you're not going to have fun in the bedroom." Along those lines, "my husband and I calendar mini-honeymoons no less than once a year—if possible a weekend together about four times a year. What creative solutions to problems and new ideas for work all happen in a setting of love with all other interruptions put aside!"

In addition to these concepts, Robert and Arvella have outlined numerous guidelines that summarize what they have learned from each other during their years together.

1. You will never forget the first time you have sex, therefore, save it for each other, as your first marriage experience together.
2. Married persons enjoy sex more, because sex is more than merely physical satisfaction.
3. Eternal secrets shared in confidence and security release deeper joys!
4. Sex becomes more fun as the years pass.
5. Compliment your lover *always!*
6. Respect each other *always!*
7. Don't take sex too seriously; relax, enjoy, and laugh with each other.
8. The greatest personal pleasure is giving your marriage partner great joy.
9. Exciting pleasures erupt with greater passion when released from the negative subconscious emotions such as fear and guilt over exposure.

10. A spiritual climate will put a halo around the sexual climax; it is the icing on the cake.

An Unexpected Visitor

During all the years Robert and Arvella have been a team, they've conquered many obstacles in their joint career. Together they overcame the doubters and negative press with the first walk-in/drive-in church and later with the Crystal Cathedral. They somehow remained free from serious problems with their family. In 1978 this family tranquillity ended. Over the next few years, tragedy struck the Schuller family, and not just once but three times.

News of the first tragedy came on Saturday, July 7, 1978, when Dr. and Mrs. Schuller were in Seoul, Korea. They were completing a three-week ministry to the Orient when they were told their thirteen-year-old daughter Carol had been severely injured in a motorcycle accident while visiting relatives in Iowa. "Her left leg has been partially amputated," they were told. "Further amputation may be necessary. We cannot say her life is out of danger. She is still in surgery."

The fear of the unknown immediately attacked the Schullers. That fear proved to be the greatest test of Arvella's positive faith. She now struggled with the pain of human grief as she took the long flight over the Pacific back to the United States. "There is no sleep," Arvella wrote in her diary. "I close my eyes but over-and-over again, all I can see is Carol lying in the dark in a ditch in terrible pain. If only I could have been with her . . ."

It would be almost twenty-four hours before Arvella would be with her pain-ridden daughter—twenty-four long hours. Finally, after arriving in Los Angeles and transferring to a specially chartered jet, Robert and Arvella arrived in Iowa and were rushed through the deserted streets to the hospital. As Arvella hurried to Carol's side, she did what most mothers do when their children are hurting—she hugged her daughter. Carol cried out in pain. Arvella jerked back, and she and Robert stumbled over each other with apologies.

The Schullers were then informed of Carol's condition. "We thought she was gone! You are fortunate to have your daughter." Arvella was thankful that her daughter's life had been spared, yet her fear continued when she learned that more of Carol's leg might have to be amputated. "God, please don't let that happen! Don't let my little girl lose any more!" she whispered fervently. "You saved her life . . . please, now save her leg."

The Schullers decided to bring Carol back to California for her next surgery. Arvella remembers that the flight was more difficult than she expected. Within the special plane there was no room to move about as Arvella sat next to Carol, holding her daughter's hand. And there was that odor coming from Carol's leg. Arvella felt as though she would become physically ill. Deep down, Arvella's fear continued: "Would Carol lose the rest of her leg?"

After extensive medical care, Carol's leg was finally amputated above the knee. Carol was going to be okay, and the Schullers celebrated with thanks. They soon realized, however, that Carol's recovery would be long and painstaking.

"Day after day, week after week, month after month: the monotony would be unbearable," writes Carol, "if it had not been for the many people who cared." During those months of recovery, no one was more important or cared more than her mother, Arvella.

"My mom was almost too helpful—not for me, but for her own health. She was incredible. She would do all her office work at the hospital room. She would be there about every day, and that was for eight months. She was always there. And then when I came home, people were saying I should have had a nurse to help take care of me, because I was really weak—but I wanted my mom."

Our Carol's story is the greatest example I can give of the benefits of a family's immersing their children—from day one—in positive thinking, positive talking, and positive actions.

ARVELLA SCHULLER

Arvella's close associate Trudi Amerikhanian remembers the struggle Arvella went through as she nursed her daughter back to health. "Those were rock-bottom times. There were times when I saw her and I thought to myself, 'Oh gosh, if you don't get yourself together, Arvella, you're going to go.' I'm sure she was experiencing every pain that Carol was experiencing. But she's a fighter; she's a survivor."

Those rock-bottom times are well remembered by Arvella. "Depression and frustration began to creep into my attitude and became a new enemy for me to cope with. Again and again I would pray it through and receive help and guidance from God—often it came through a friend. God's little miracles day by day continued to come our way."

Arvella was not alone in her concern for Carol. The shock of the accident had an intense effect on the entire Schuller family. Like most struggles, it brought everyone closer together—almost everyone.

The second unexpected family trouble affected son Robert, the founding pastor of Rancho Capistrano Community Church in Southern California. His ten-year marriage ended, devastatingly, in divorce. "It was a terrible thing for them," says Marge Kelley, "a terrible blow. Dr. Schuller talks all the time about one husband and wife, and if you get married you're married forever. Bob's divorce was hard on the family because they're very family-oriented."

Although Arvella felt the pain of her son's struggles, she refused to interfere where she wasn't invited. "She tried to see both sides . . . and tried to be loving," says Marge.

"Both Dr. and Mrs. Schuller were very supportive. They didn't at any point that I could see try to interfere."

On January 8, 1984, Robert A. Schuller announced to his congregation that his wife had filed for divorce. In his best-selling book *Getting Through the Going-Through Stage,* Bob writes: "It has been devastating for me. I know that we especially need God's love and your support to carry us through our personal going-through stage. Please pray for us."

THE STRESS OF CARING

Before that January day in 1984, Arvella had faced her third struggle. This one was much more personal and life-threatening, not this time to Carol, but to Arvella herself. In 1979 she discovered that she had cancer. A year after Carol's accident Arvella noticed she had a lump in her breast. She had monthly tests, yet the lump continued to grow. Finally the doctor performed a biopsy. The lump was malignant, and immediately Arvella had a mastectomy.

As she lay in her hospital bed, Arvella's mind reviewed her struggle with Carol's accident. While she endured that long flight from Korea to California, Arvella originally wrote: "There are no thoughts of guilt, and I am surprised. Often I had feelings of guilt as I left the children for a trip with my husband." Now she wondered if she "was angry or bitter way down in my subconscious? There might be guilt feelings so deep I could not touch them now."

A friend's letter added to her concern. "Arvella," she wrote, "I think you brought the cancer on yourself. Either you felt guilty because you were not with Carol at the time of the accident, or you . . . subconsciously blamed God." Daughter Carol cites a corollary cause. "I think part of it had to do with all the stress, because it was a lot of work. She was wonderful and she never complained."

Regardless of the cause, Arvella has always had the faith to overcome adversity. "That's why I call her a tower of strength," says Mrs. Norman Vincent Peale. "She went through those situations and had a depth of spiritual belief and practice whereby she could gain what she needed to overcome those problems. . . ." Since her operation, all of Arvella's biopsies have been negative.

THE SCHULLER TEAM TODAY

The tragedies that struck Oral and Evelyn Roberts and Robert and Arvella Schuller have had much of the same lasting impact on the two women. Of the Robertses' struggles, daughter Roberta says: "It's made my mother more interesting in some ways, more analytical, and in some ways sadder. More than anything, it affected them both in that they've worked harder."

Concerning Arvella's response to tragedy, Trudi Amerikhanian says, "I think those times make you run deeper and I've seen that in Arvella. . . . Her faith soared," yet they were still "rock-bottom times."

"It's like I said, she's like a rock. You can just see her set her course and she goes along. She has tremendous inner strength," adds Dr. Schuller's secretary.

Today Arvella's inner strength helped bring her husband's ministry to its zenith. Dr. Robert Schuller is without a doubt the most successful author writing for both "Christian" and "secular" audiences. And "The Hour of Power" is the highest-rated Christian broadcast offering a complete Sunday worship service.

Certainly more important for the Schullers is the present "success" of their family. Son Robert is happily remarried, with a new child. As in the case of Oral Roberts and his son Richard, some insiders wonder if Robert A. Schuller is being prepared to assume his father's role in "The Hour of Power." Time will tell. Daughter Carol also recently married and is expecting her first child in 1987.

For Arvella, the Dutch girl with the stick-to-itive nature, all of these successes start with the basics. For her, the basics in life are a positive attitude and making the right choices. "Never, never, never be negative," writes Arvella Schuller. "Are you excited about the family? I am! Are you excited about life? I am! Are you excited about yourself? I am!

"You can make a decision now to start building a positive family today, even if your dreams have been shattered, or hopes have turned to ashes. Happiness is a choice. Choose to be positive and you choose the success attitude in family, home, career—all of living."

FRANCES SWAGGART

❧⟡❧

Some have said that I'm a charismatic leader—I don't know if I am or not. But this I do know. I probably would have quit had it not been for my wife. What we have been able to do for the Lord could not have been done without her. It's that simple.

JIMMY SWAGGART

Whether you are sitting downstairs in the lobby, waiting on the second floor in the executive offices, or talking to him a thousand miles away on the phone, it's that voice that you'll always remember. It has a resonance that carries, that flows over you. Before you ever see him, you hear him. It's almost always been that way. And you can feel his presence. Actually it's quite unusual, but at the same time warm and inviting—and very different from the intensity you feel from television.

As you climb the stairs to the second floor, you pass the "Living Wall" of stones; each rock represents a major donation to the ministry. At the top of the stairs are the executive offices. Once inside, you first notice the gold records. There are twelve in all, representing Jimmy Swaggart's top-selling releases. He, of course, is the one with the resonant voice. He is also the one with the corner office and a phone with so many buttons "it would take a Harvard graduate to answer it."

Before you reach that corner office, you pass another. Though the voice comes from that corner, everything else in the executive suite flows to and from the other office. It's right next door to his and it's the office of Frances Swaggart. And she's not just Jimmy's wife; she's the Chief Executive Officer of the Jimmy Swaggart Ministries.

JIMMY AND HIS MUSIC

Frances Anderson first met Jimmy Swaggart in church where he and his famous rock-and-roll cousin, Jerry Lee Lewis, were playing the piano. "He had a touch and a feel to his music that was very moving," says Frances. "If he was playing a fast song, it was impossible to keep from clapping your hands; if he was playing a slow piece, it would move you to tears."

Music and that inviting voice have always played a large part in the success of Jimmy Swaggart. To date, he has sold more than fifteen million records, including his three most famous—"God Took Away My Yesterdays," taped in 1962; "This Is Just What Heaven Means to Me," taped with the Nashville Sounds; and "There Is a River," which stayed number one in America longer than any other gospel song.

Frances is quick to admit the role music has played in her husband's success. "When my husband made his first album and his records started to be played over the radio stations, that increased the number of people that knew about Jimmy Swaggart. People have bought millions of his records and this is the way people outside of the Assemblies of God started coming to our meeting. It was through his records that the word got out. On his own, with his music and his ability, Jimmy could have had a terrific lifestyle; but he put that second. When God called him to preach, he put that first."

Preaching the Gospel is first, but music is definitely the second most powerful force in the world.

FRANCES SWAGGART

A Powerful Force

If music is the second most powerful force, there is a good chance that Frances Swaggart is third. Preaching, music, and Frances—it would be no stretch of the imagination to say this is the exact order of things you'll find in the Jimmy Swaggart Ministries. Make no mistake about it: Frances Swaggart is a powerful force.

"I'm not a weakling," says Frances. "I don't keel over and pass out at opposition. In fact, I act the opposite. When I meet an obstacle, I don't turn and run . . . rather, I'm determined to overcome it." Only son Donnie agrees with his mother's evaluation of herself. "My mother is very tough," says Donnie. "Not in the sense of being emotionally hard or callous, but in the sense of discipline. She is probably the most disciplined person that I've ever been around in my life."

Her evangelist husband, Jimmy, sees Frances's unassuming strength as a sort of "ace in the hole." "My wife is a very pretty lady. Of course, I'm prejudiced, but she looks about ten years younger than she is." Partly because of her looks, few people think Frances wields the power she does. "I think that's a plus," says Jimmy, "because a lot of people think they have a pushover and they have real problems on their hands. You ask any of the fifteen hundred employees and they know; they understand. But the person who watches the telecast would have little or scant knowledge of her responsibilities."

Frances's motto: "Whenever you have problems, you learn to overcome them, to solve them, to knock the door down or do whatever."

Everyone agrees that Frances gained her personal strength from her mother. "My mother was the most influential person in my life. There are just some things that she instilled in me that I have not forgotten today and never will forget." Frances's older brother, Bob, says, "My mother was real independent. She did whatever she had to do. She worked in the fields, she picked cotton, she walked to town to buy groceries. That may not be the way you perceive Frances to be, but she is independent to a certain degree. When she is right, she doesn't give up."

Frances Anderson grew up on a forty-two-acre farm about two miles outside of Wisner, Louisiana. In addition to her older brother, Bob, she has two sisters, Linda and Peggy. Today Bob is a top executive in the Jimmy Swaggart Ministries—reporting to his sister Frances—and Linda is Jimmy's personal secretary. Few memories remain from those early days except Bob's. "I used to use Frances and my other sister, Peggy, to practice football with. I made them do the tackling and the blocking. I ran over them a lot. I tell Frances that's the reason she is getting back at me now. She's finally got the upper hand."

While Mrs. Anderson taught her children to be tough, their father was not that driven; rather, "he would take things as they came." The reason was alcohol; Frances's father was an alcoholic. It's a memory Frances prefers not to discuss. "I don't like to be too negative. I grew up in an alcoholic's home. I know all the problems and I can relate to children in that environment today. That's why I hate alcohol. Any preacher that wants to say it's all right to drink, I'd love to wring his neck."

QUESTIONS OF LOVE

Jimmy vividly recalls the first time he saw his wife-to-be. "I was in church seated about two-thirds of the way back on the left-hand side as you come in the door. She was in the choir. My sister had described her to me, and that's the way

I was able to recognize her. The moment I saw her I fell head over heels in love."

It wasn't long before he was ready to marry Frances. She, however, had reservations. "Never ever, growing up, did I ever think, hope, pray, or remotely think . . . that I would be a minister's wife. Now, I dreamed of everything else, but I was not raised in church, so this lifestyle was not in my thinking." Frances's parents were equally uncomfortable with the idea of their marriage, as were Jimmy's. "Do you realize what you're doing?" asked his mother. His father wanted to know, "How are you going to make a living?"

There was one person who had a keener eye on Frances's future—her uncle. "You're going to wind up marrying that preacher's son," he told her. Frances would snap back, "That's not true"; but in three months it was true and the couple were married.

It wasn't an easy wedding to pull off. First Frances's parents refused their permission. Then Jimmy's father, who was a Pentecostal minister, refused to marry them. Finally Jimmy found a Baptist preacher to perform the wedding, but only after he borrowed his mother's ring for the ceremony. When the ceremony ended, Jimmy took Frances to her home and he went to his. It wasn't until the next day that Jimmy explained the situation to Frances's parents.

The young couple moved in temporarily with Jimmy's parents until he could find work. As Jimmy writes in his autobiography: "It was a frustrating time. The one time in my life when I should have been the happiest, I was the most miserable."

A VOICE OF THE FUTURE

Something was to happen soon that would change their lives.

Frances was in the kitchen talking with Jimmy's mother, who said, "The Lord called Jimmy into the ministry when he was eight years old, and he will never be able to escape that call. One day he's going to preach the Gospel." She continued to tell Frances all the things she felt the Lord had told her. In the middle of the conversation Frances heard another voice. "Just as I'm speaking to you right now, it was a voice . . . not an audible voice, but a spoken message to my spirit. And it said, 'Yes, I've called Jimmy and it's a special call and it's going to be very, very difficult. I have put you with him. You can be a help or a hindrance. If you ever stand in his way, I'll remove you and replace you with someone else.' "

> *The Lord said to me, "He will not be just a pastor, he will not be just a preacher, he will not be just an evangelist. He has a special call."*
>
> FRANCES SWAGGART

That voice terrified young Frances. "I was sitting shaking in that chair and I didn't know what was happening to me. It was like something was unveiled in front of my eyes. I thought maybe I had lost my mind." She decided not to tell anyone—not Jimmy, not her mother-in-law. She was afraid they might think she was misguided or "crazy." More important was her love for her new husband; she wanted to wait and see what would unfold. She loved Jimmy and was willing to do whatever he was called to do. "That's my attitude," says Frances, "and always has been."

Soon things did start happening. The first thing was Frances and Jimmy's total commitment to their faith. It happened at an old-fashioned Assembly of God revival three months after their wedding. "We went to the altar together. I accepted the Lord and Jimmy rededicated his life," said Frances. "I cried a lot, I really didn't understand what had happened to me." Since she'd been raised a Methodist, the intense emotion of the experience was new to her.

Six months after Jimmy finally surrendered to God, this young preacher's son was ready to follow in his father's footsteps. He felt the time was right. "I've got something I want to do Saturday," he told Frances, "and I want you to help me. I'm going to have a street service in Mangham." Her reply was simple and straightforward. "Sure, whatever you want me to do."

That first service brought a small crowd of fifteen to twenty people. Jimmy's hands and knees were trembling and his collar was soaking with sweat, but he kept on. In ten minutes he preached everything he knew—twice. From that Saturday on, every weekend Jimmy preached anywhere he could. Soon he moved up from just street services to using a flatbed truck with microphones and loudspeakers.

Hundreds gathered to hear the new evangelist, yet because offerings were small, Jimmy kept his part-time job with the Louisiana Soil Conservation Department. It wasn't until five years later, in January 1958, that Jimmy would leave the security of his job to enter evangelistic work full-time. He held his first full-fledged revival in Sterlington, Louisiana.

The fourth night of that first revival, Jimmy became deathly ill with pneumonia. The doctor bills began to mount. There was no money, and little hope. Jimmy remembers lying in that hospital bed: "All of a sudden it seemed the room was sinking, as if it were an elevator going down a shaft, down, down. It seemed as if all the darkened, oppressive forces of hell had been unleashed against me."

In time Jimmy had finally had enough. In a hoarse voice he shouted, "Lord, you're with me. I don't know how you'll take care of me, but I trust you to do it. I have done what you told me to do, and I'm going to receive my healing." Within months Jimmy was back on the road.

MOTELS, BASEMENTS AND OLD CARS

Before Jimmy's first revival meeting, there was an earlier life-changing event in the Swaggart family. Frances gave birth to Donnie, their first—and only—child.

With a newborn baby in the family, full-time evangelistic work became even more difficult. "It got very discouraging. Back in the early years, tremendously discouraging," says Frances. Their small family traveled from one small church to another, then returned home to pray for another meeting—and enough money to pay the bills. Perhaps the toughest times were when Donnie became ill. If Jimmy was due to hold another meeting, Frances would have no choice but to bundle up Donnie in the back of the car. The three of them would keep driving down the highway. "Jimmy and I wouldn't speak," says Frances; "we felt so guilty about raising him that way. We never had another child."

Donnie, too, remembers.

"I was a child and we were on the road full-time, Dad going from church to church preaching. We lived in cheap motels or in the basements of churches. We'd get to a new place and my mother would go shopping for food and disinfectant to clean up an area where we ate and slept. The bathroom always seemed to be down the hall."

After Donnie and his mother spent the day together, it was time for the evening service. At night "she became 'the preacher's wife,' mixing with the congregation, selling Dad's records. And then it was time to move on to the next church. A great deal of our life was spent in old cars. The first time we stayed in a Holiday Inn, I thought we were in the Taj Mahal," says Donnie.

One of the difficulties of raising Donnie on the road was his education. For the first four years Frances taught Donnie using teaching materials from the Calvert Correspondence School of Baltimore. Each school day she would give him at least eight hours of instruction. Later he went to public school—or schools. "I went to thirty-one public schools. It was a little difficult at first, getting used to school. I'd spend three weeks in one place and eight weeks in another place. I started changing schools in the fourth grade."

Frances likes to stress the advantages of Donnie's on-the-road education. "He got to travel all over the nation, meet different types of people, and learn how to move and operate in a different situation every few weeks."

Regardless of the struggles, moving from school to school was easier than having his mother teach him. "I mean, she was tough," says Donnie. "I remember the first time I went to public school was here in Baton Rouge. We came home for a short period of rest and she took me over to Brownsfield Elementary. At the time we didn't have a home. Our lodging consisted of two bedrooms in my grandfather's house. Coming home from school, I remember my first reaction. 'This is so easy compared to my mother. This is a breeze; anybody can do this.'"

According to Jimmy, their life on the road "is almost a book within itself; it's a study in patience and endurance." To understand how Frances handled the struggle, "you have to understand a little something about her," says the evangelist. "She was not raised in a Pentecostal church. She was raised in a Methodist church. So she knew absolutely nothing about what she was to become. It was a totally different world for her. Yet all of those years, she never complained once. I'll be honest with you, I probably would have quit if it had not been for her. She provided me with courage and fortitude."

A wife can be his best critic; she can also be the strongest encourager. You can't go overboard either way. I think a man needs that.

FRANCES SWAGGART

Like Arvella Schuller, Frances is committed to a positive approach to marriage, especially for ministers' families. "I've seen some ministers' wives who have stayed on the negative side and never gotten past that point. That is pathetic, because a woman can either make or break a man's ministry. You can help your husband excel or you can hold him back. Some of it is on his part, but . . . you can make or break a man."

Frances stresses that a wife should have more than just a positive outlook—an active faith of her own. "I think a wife has to have a walk with God herself, where the Lord can speak to her. When I feel the witness in my spirit, then I know that God is speaking to my husband. The biggest thing a wife can do is to know that the Lord can speak to her as well as her husband."

RECORDS AND RADIO

A turning point in the Swaggart ministry came when Jimmy recorded his first record. Frances was there to be certain it was a success; like her mother, she would do whatever it took. Jimmy, however, had his doubts. "Being a musician, I knew all the flaws that were in the album. It sounded terrible to me. Besides I kept telling her, 'Why would the deejays want to play my record, when they have the Blackwood Brothers, the Happy Goodmans, and the Statesmen? They don't know me, they've never heard of me.' But she kept on, she kept pounding and pounding. She saw something in it that I evidently didn't see."

Frances recalls, "We argued about that record until the Lord took it out of my hands and Jimmy's. A deejay accidentally got hold of one and started playing it on a station near Detroit, in Pontiac, Michigan. It went over like house afire. People started calling in and ordering it by the hundreds. We couldn't comprehend it. In that particular case, I was right."

In 1969 Frances again stood her ground to keep alive a new direction in Jimmy's ministry. On January 1 of that year, the ministry launched a new radio program. Jimmy named it the "Camp Meeting Hour"; Frances felt the name had "a real down-home touch." For months Jimmy made tapes and shipped them to the participating stations. All of his money from revival meetings and record sales was poured into the new radio effort. Yet as he remembers, "the response was poor, very poor. In fact, the response was practically zero." He decided it was time to cancel the program.

"No one knew who we were," says Jimmy, "and I didn't know what to do. Once again I think I would have quit; I think I would have stopped." But Frances would have none of it.

In detail she remembers those trying times. "I didn't want to go on radio to begin with. We had been traveling for years . . . and had just recently built our home in Baton Rouge. We kind of had plans to settle down. At that time radio ministers didn't have a good name, and I could see us being put in that category. So I wasn't in favor of it at first. But he went ahead, and rightly so. After a short period of time, I sensed in my spirit that the radio ministry was God's will. I guess I didn't realize how important it was."

When Jimmy finally told Frances he was canceling the program, she answered him firmly, "God told us to go on radio. . . . If we have to sell the furniture in the house, we'll do it to stay on." Frances was unyielding and Jimmy knew she was right.

> *I can honestly say that in every crisis this ministry has faced . . . almost without exception, her advice has always been the best advice.*
>
> DONNIE SWAGGART

Regardless of Frances's urgings, Jimmy continued with his plans to cancel the "Camp Meeting Hour." Before the program finally went off the air, one of the broadcasters preempted the taped program and went on the air. He told the listeners that Jimmy Swaggart was canceling the program because of the lack of response. "Folks, I don't feel the program should be canceled," he insisted, "and even if Brother Swaggart wants to cancel, I'll play the same tapes over and over until they wear out. If you want the program to stay on, I want you to write him."

Write him they did. Three days later, Frances found a U.S. mailbag on her front porch. After opening the bag, she ran to the phone to call her husband. "I've got something to tell you," she announced. "Over nine hundred letters and something like three thousand dollars came in the mail today for the program." Jimmy was so stunned that he began to cry. Once again Frances's faith had held fast. Equally important was the change that took place in Jimmy at that time. From that point on, Jimmy Swaggart believed in his call and his future.

FRANCES: CORPORATE EXECUTIVE

Success has been with the Swaggart ministry for the last three decades. Today Jimmy Swaggart's face is the most recognized of any religious leader in America except Billy Graham's. Besides Jimmy, the person who has done the most to make that happen is none other than Frances.

Jimmy still makes the major decisions, and Donnie is chief of staff with five hundred people under him; but it is Frances who really runs the Jimmy Swaggart Ministries. Though she shies away from the title, Jimmy says she's "the CEO, Chief Executive Officer, for the organization. When you consider we employ about fifteen hundred people, and we're involved in 191 countries of the world with the telecast aired in 143 . . . you can imagine the magnitude of her responsibility."

> *People would be most surprised to learn that I play as large a role in the ministry as I do. I work in every phase of the ministry and everybody answers to me. I know where all the money goes. I get reports every day, and I go through every one.*

FRANCES SWAGGART

Donnie's office is within fifteen yards of his mother's. Over the years he has worked his way up the ministry ladder and has had the opportunity to observe how his mother works alongside his famous father. "My mother is very level-headed. She sees both sides of the picture almost instantly, whereas Dad works on emotion. He is an artist and a musician; they have a temperament that is a little different than anybody else's. He feels things.

"Secondly," continues Donnie, "my mother is very perceptive of people. She can spot a phony twenty miles away. It doesn't matter how much sugar and spice is flowing, she can always spot a phony. And she can cut through wasted talk faster than anybody that I have ever seen."

Along with finance and marketing, personnel is one of Frances's specialties. "She is level-headed and yet very tough. She will not let outside situations distract her from what she knows is right even if it means hurting people's feelings. No matter how difficult the decision, she will not pass it off to somebody else." When she is dealing with a problem employee, she might approach the situation by saying, "We want to do the best for you, but you are not acting right and we're not going to tolerate it. I love you, but you are not going to work here anymore."

According to Donnie, the best example of Frances's abilities was how she handled the ministry's early relationship with the media. "When the ministry began to takeoff and get attention, the media began to take notice, but it was all negative. To them everything we did had an ulterior motive behind it. We would have a reporter come in and interview us, and then go back and write a totally opposite report. It looked like some of the most powerful media forces were out to get us."

At the time, Jimmy felt the best way to deal with the media was to bare his soul, present the facts, and treat reporters fairly. Unfortunately, many members of the press continued to write biased, negative articles. "My mother saw through that game much quicker than he did," says

Donnie. "She helped formulate a lot of victories. Since then we have seen somewhat of a turnaround with the media. She's been one of the reasons for it. She was very tough in dealing with them and very up front."

> *I always say to the Lord, "Before he takes me to heaven, let me have it with the reporters." Yet more and more some reporters are trying to give an unbiased report. In the past it was always biased.*
>
> FRANCES SWAGGART

Frances is keenly aware of the power that her husband's television popularity offers. "The news media is not used to having a minister with a platform such as ministers have today. It's been kind of a little monopoly. They've been the ones that reported the news . . . and given the American public what they wanted to hear. Now, through the ministry, television preachers have that same platform. I think that bothers them."

Along with that power comes the opportunity for television evangelists to involve themselves in politics. Frances, however, is dead set against it. "I do not feel it's a minister's place to involve himself in politics, such as running for a public office. The calling of God is the greatest call that he could ever receive. He should never let anything interfere with telling the story of Christ."

Jimmy agrees. "I don't believe in ministers being in politics. I think it's wrong." Yet he offers some qualifications. "I believe that Christians ought to be very involved in politics." He also believes "there are a lot of good men that are tremendously talented that serve the Lord" but aren't limited by a calling of evangelism or pastoring.

One such person is Pat Robertson. Both Frances and Jimmy decided early to support Pat Robertson, yet Frances admits there were mixed feelings. She was leery of a Robertson candidacy because of the problems it might cause for other television evangelists. "I would definitely prefer for him not to run, because I feel it's going to cause trouble for television ministries in general," says Frances.

The Ministry "Explodes"

In 1981 the Swaggart ministry really took off. "We were going along, doing everything we had always done," says Donnie, "and all of a sudden somebody pulled open the blinds, the light hit us, and we just exploded across the nation." According to Jimmy, the reason behind the sudden popularity was the difference between radio and television. "Radio is like a rifle, television is like a shotgun. Well, I'll put it this way, television is like a huge burst out of a shotgun."

When Jimmy Swaggart went on television five years earlier, there was little response. "We didn't have our own production unit, we didn't have anything. We just taped our own crusades and did some studio tapings. People on the Coast put them together. They were put together badly."

Eventually the ministry established its own production unit. "After that we started editing our own programs and putting them together. At that time the ministry exploded. We were finally able to put on the screen what should be put on the screen."

At the same time the Swaggarts expanded the telecast outside the United States. They put all their energies into foreign missions, including building churches and schools and providing children with clothes and food. Today, with a monthly budget of more than $1.5 million, these services are provided through "Childcare International," the nation's largest church-related children's ministry.

Frances spends most of the time at her office reviewing the many ministry activities and planning for the future. During the years she has worked in the ministry she has done almost every job, including wrapping phonograph records. One of those early tasks she continues to this day is reviewing the mail. It comes in all types: compliments, requests for books and records, desperate pleas for help—and always there are the critics. Yet criticism is one thing the Swaggarts have never shied away from. In fact, sometimes Frances will walk right into it.

Frances also plays an active role in the crusade services. Often she makes an appearance on the platform before her husband begins to minister. For the most part, however, the evangelist's wife is busiest behind the scenes. Like Ruth Graham and Evelyn Roberts, she serves as her husband's closest adviser and strongest supporter. After the service she knows Jimmy will ask her, "How was the message?" or "What did you think of the music?" Frances is always ready with careful observations and constructive comments.

For Jimmy the crusade services are the high point of his life. Interestingly enough, the part that moves him the most is the introduction. When asked "What part of the ministry is most meaningful to you?" he replied, "It would be when Donnie says, 'Ladies and Gentlemen, this is my dad, your evangelist, Jimmy Swaggart.' "

It's not that Jimmy likes to hear his name; rather, it's that he knows it's finally time to do what he's been called to do. "I am an evangelist, that's the call of God in my heart. And when you see thousands and thousands of people sitting there and you're about to deliver a message that you believe God has given you . . . you tremble inside.

"Paul described it in his letter to the Church at Corinth," adds the evangelist. " 'I came to you with much weakness, fear, and trembling.' That pretty well describes it; you tremble inside. Especially when you realize that same service is being taped and will later be shown in 143 countries of the world and translated into some thirteen languages." In 1987 the Jimmy Swaggart Team has scheduled twelve crusades, with four in the United States and eight in foreign countries.

FRANCES AND JIMMY AT HOME

Every day Jimmy spends hours in his study preparing his messages. Even though he devotes so much time to prayer and study, Frances seldom feels neglected. "I'm self-sufficient and he's self-sufficient," says Frances. "I never make him think he's neglecting me." In many ways Jimmy agrees, yet he adds, "If I have to go somewhere without her, it's like part of me is missing. I never get bored with her. She's always extremely interesting."

Because of their busy schedules, Frances and Jimmy are not able to spend enough time at their new home. Frances remembers the many discussions she and Jimmy went through as it was being constructed. When first asked about the type of house she wanted, she replied, "I want a house, but I don't want any walls except what has to be there to hold it up. I want just as much glass as could be put on it, and I want it plain in front. One little door is all I want."

Frances was tired of the criticism other evangelists were receiving about their homes. She didn't want those stories told of her. She wanted something real simple.

But Jimmy wanted columns. The plans were quickly redrawn.

The Swaggarts first saw their new home upon returning from a crusade to Africa. "All of a sudden my house sprang up in front of me," says Frances, "and I didn't know what to do." As she viewed the new front of their house, she couldn't keep from laughing. Finally, in a burst of laughter, she turned to her husband and said, "You got your columns."

At home the Swaggarts spend their time talking about the ministry and simply enjoying each other's company. "We're very compatible," says Frances, "and we love each other dearly. It's been a very strong marriage." Jimmy adds, "I've never had a family problem. We could have, we would have, if she had been a different type of person. She's very understanding. And we enjoy each other's company. What one likes the other likes." They also enjoy relaxing with their grandchildren.

One reason Frances and Jimmy get along so well has to be their laughter. Both have a strong sense of humor. Jimmy's secretary is convinced that her boss's sense of humor will surprise most people. "Jimmy's very intense about what he does, but he's also a lot of fun," says Linda. Because of the telecast many people think Jimmy Swaggart is hard and unyielding. The evangelist adds, "I talk to people that see us on television and they think we're going to come riding in on a horse and brandishing a sword."

One of his indulgences is hamburgers. "They are my favorite," says Jimmy. "Recently when we were coming out of Atlanta after having just closed a crusade, I stopped at a Krystal and ordered four hamburgers. That's better than the finest steak you could make in the best steak house in the country." Frances's appetite is different. "I'm into diets," she says. "I have to lean on Jimmy hard. Dieting lasts one day with him." Frances also enjoys jogging. She was at one time running four miles a day.

FRANCES AND JIMMY TODAY

In 1987 Frances receives the most joy when she's at work, serving alongside her husband in the ministry. "I'm happiest if we've had a fantastic service the night before. Regardless of how difficult it is, or how many problems we encounter, we're going to do what God has called us to do. Many times I've prayed, 'Lord, why are you allowing certain things to happen, you could help us a little more.' But I've found that you grow spiritually from all the problems."

Besides her unwaving faith in the Lord, the respect Frances has for her husband is what keeps her going. "Jimmy has tremendous drive, tremendous ability. He's highly motivated and motivated in the right direction. It's easy for me to fall in line and do whatever is necessary, because I respect him." It's her husband's preaching Frances enjoys most. "His preaching has always come first. He has the ability to communicate to people on any level. When he teaches on a certain subject, people can relate to it . . . and for the first time complicated things become understandable." Of all people, Dan Rather of CBS News agrees. "Jimmy Swaggart may be the most effective speaker in the country," he said in a July 1986 New York *Times* article.

When he preaches, Jimmy Swaggart can be highly controversial. "Jimmy's very outspoken and he's a very honest individual," says Frances. "If he feels something is right, he's got to stand up for it regardless of whether it's popular or unpopular. He's got to preach what he feels God would have him preach regardless of the cost. The stands he has had to take in the past and will have to continue to take in the future are what bring a lot of the controversy. Some people just don't want to hear what God is really saying."

That outspoken attitude has caused some people to wonder if Jimmy Swaggart is a twentieth-century prophet. When asked this question while speaking at the Jimmy Swaggart Bible College, Frances responded with a qualified yes. "I personally think he's a prophet, I'll be honest with you. I feel that he is . . . but I'm going to clarify my answer by saying God will be the final judge."

In the beginning God said he was placing a special call on Jimmy. I've never looked at him as a special person . . . but someone striving to do the will of God. The special calling of where he places my husband today, I'll have to leave up to the Lord.

FRANCES SWAGGART

What does Jimmy think of all this? "The main thing is to do the will of God," says the evangelist. "If I can do the will of God, just like Abraham Lincoln said, 'If you're wrong a thousand angels standing on a stack of Bibles swearing you're right won't make you right. If you're right it will all come out.' "

Someday, when it does "all come out," people will discover a story quite similar to this: it has been that resonant voice—the preaching voice and the singing voice of Jimmy Swaggart—that brought success. Yet it has been Frances Swaggart that kept that voice finely tuned and moving ahead. As her brother, Bob, says, "I have heard Jimmy over and over and over . . . a hundred times say that if it was not for Frances he wouldn't have had the drive and the desire to get into radio and television. If it wasn't for her he would have quit years ago."

If that voice was ever silenced—for whatever reason—how would Frances respond? Would this strong-willed yet totally feminine native Louisianian keep going? Of course she would. "We've had ups and downs in the ministry. We've all prayed together, cried together, had problems, and God's brought us through it all," she says. "To answer your question, yes, I would. And I would be down on my knees asking God where . . . and how . . . and what."